Welcome and thank you!

I hope you enjoy these amazing arachnids.

Dedicated to my dear wife Lisa Hale who lost her fear through photography.

If using markers, place a sheet of paper behind your page.

Arachnids are amazing creatures despite fear giving them a bad name. This book will bring you close to them in a safe manner while enjoying your coloring hobby. They really are worth learning about and I only wish I had learned much earlier. Be sure to check out my other coloring book titles:

Truly Bizarre

Zombie Town USA

Kitten Monsters

Freaky Creatures

MS Sucks

Goofy Dragons

Clown Warp

Wilde World of Reptiles and Amphibians

Amazing Characters

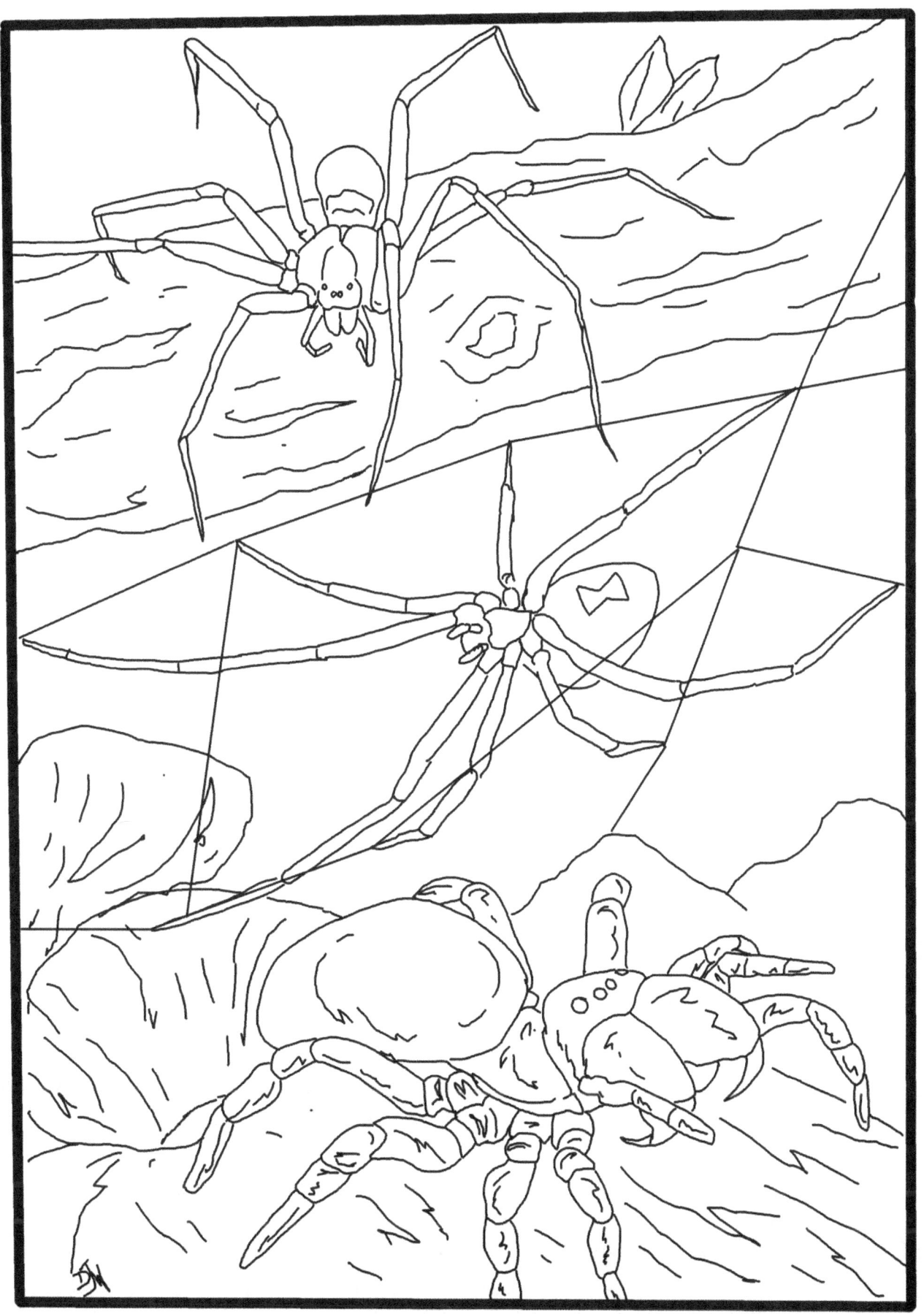

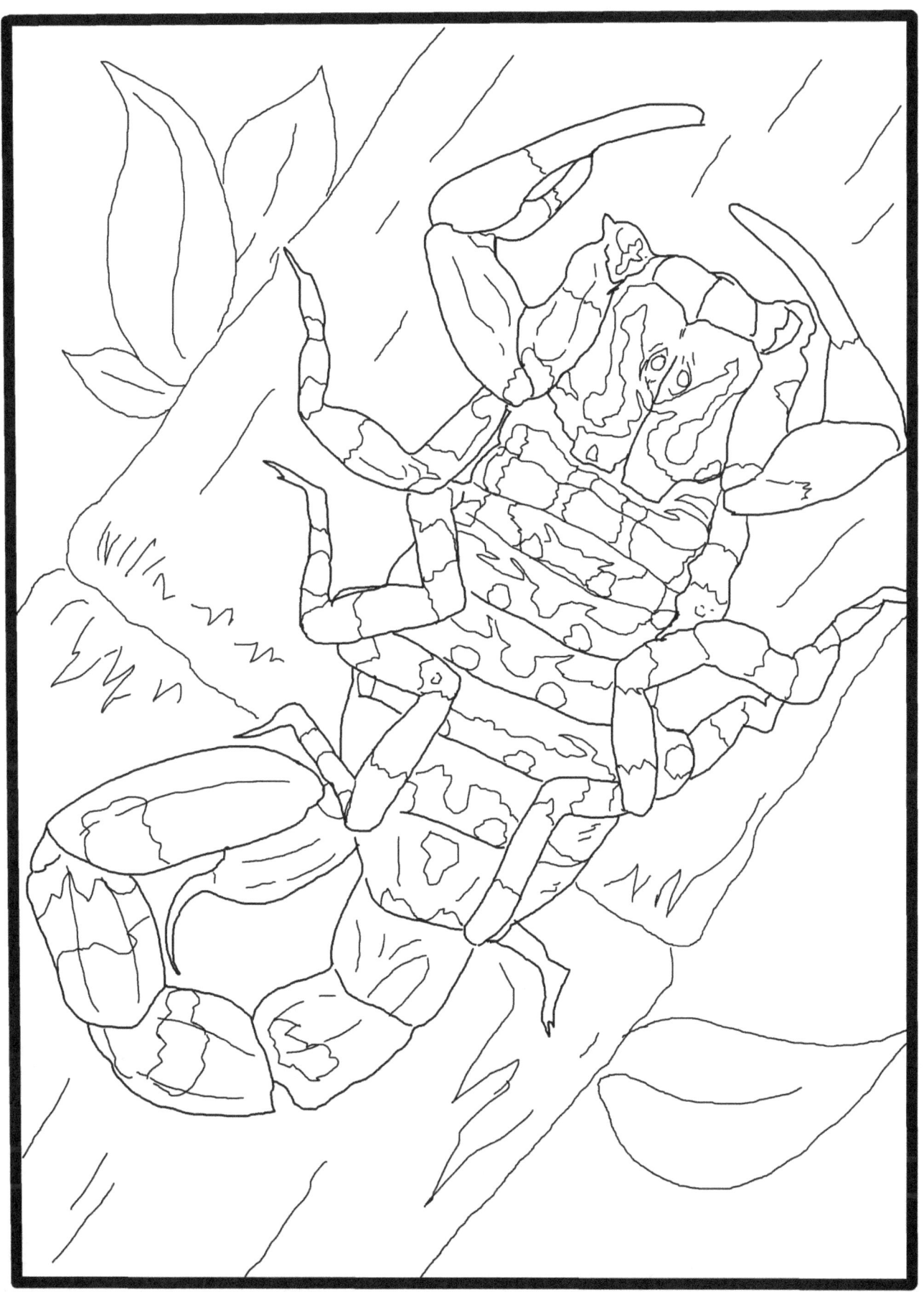

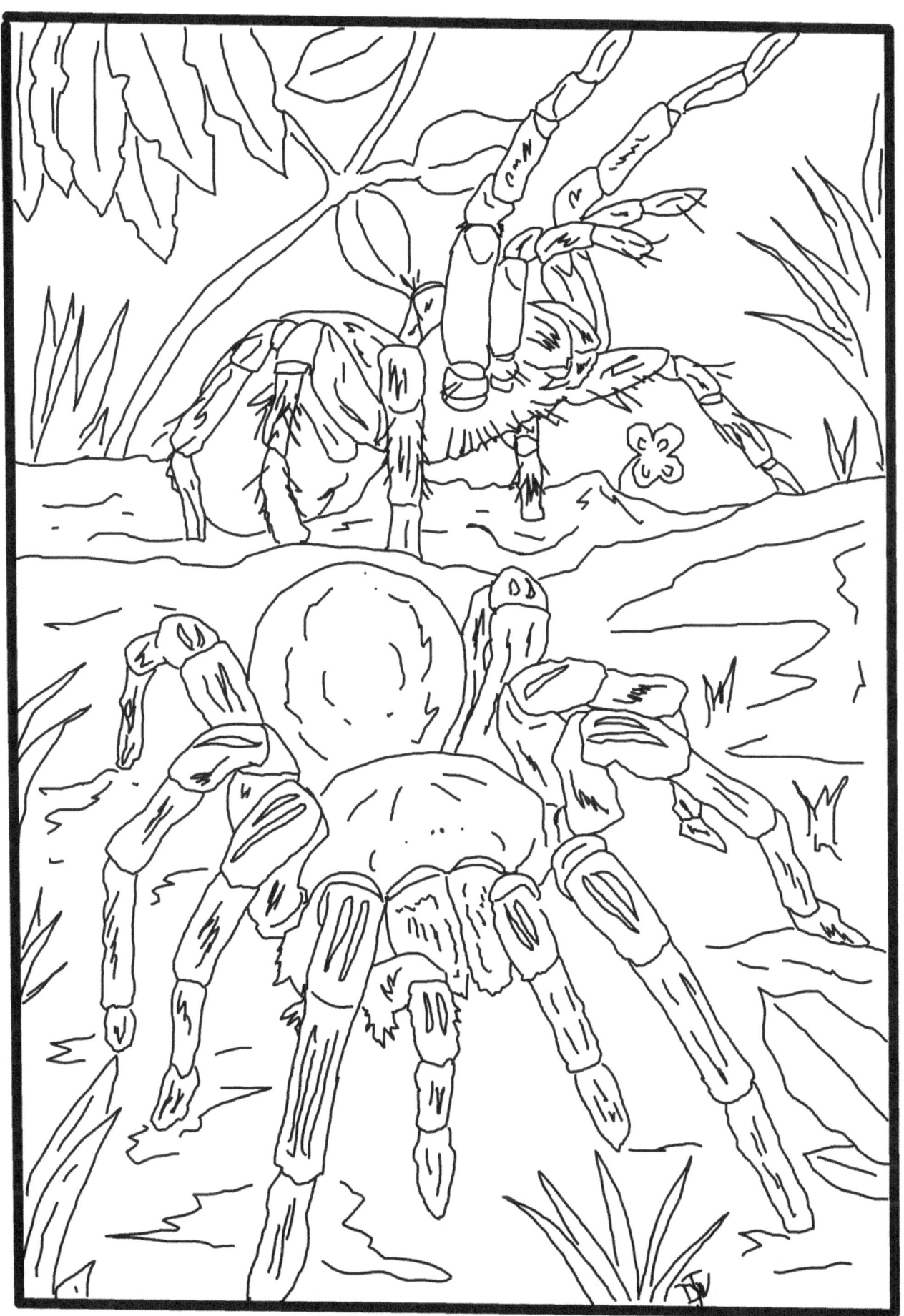

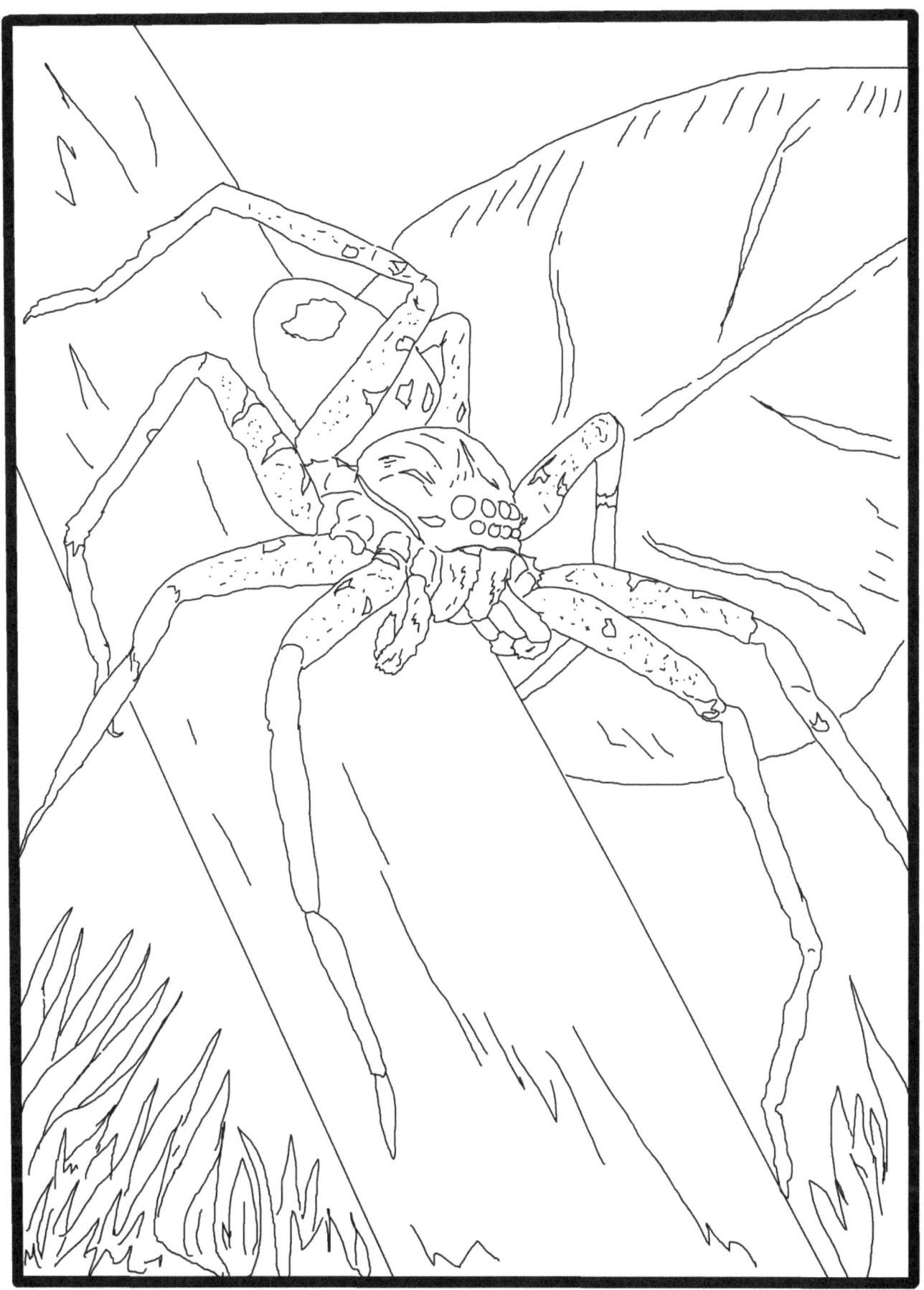

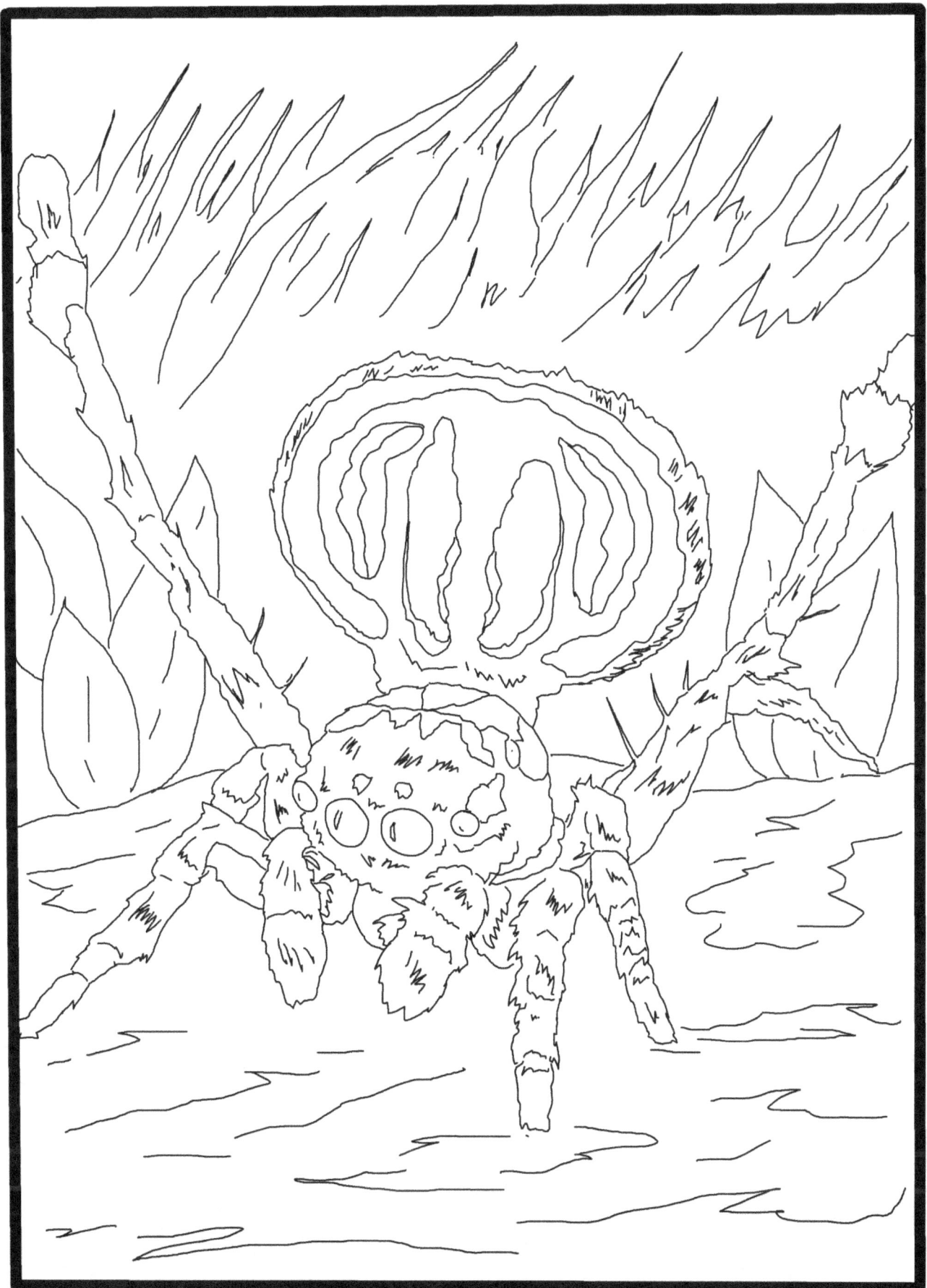

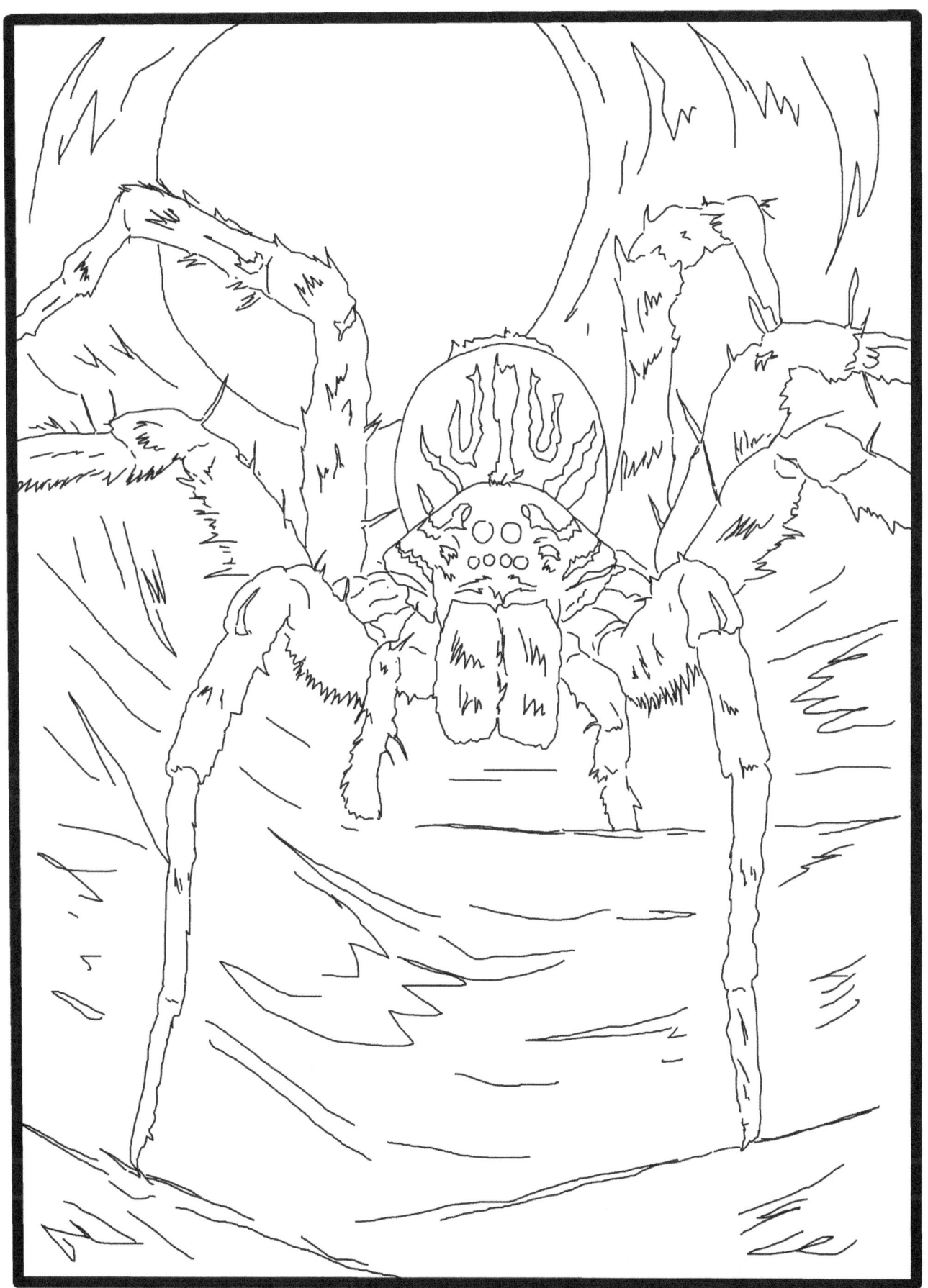

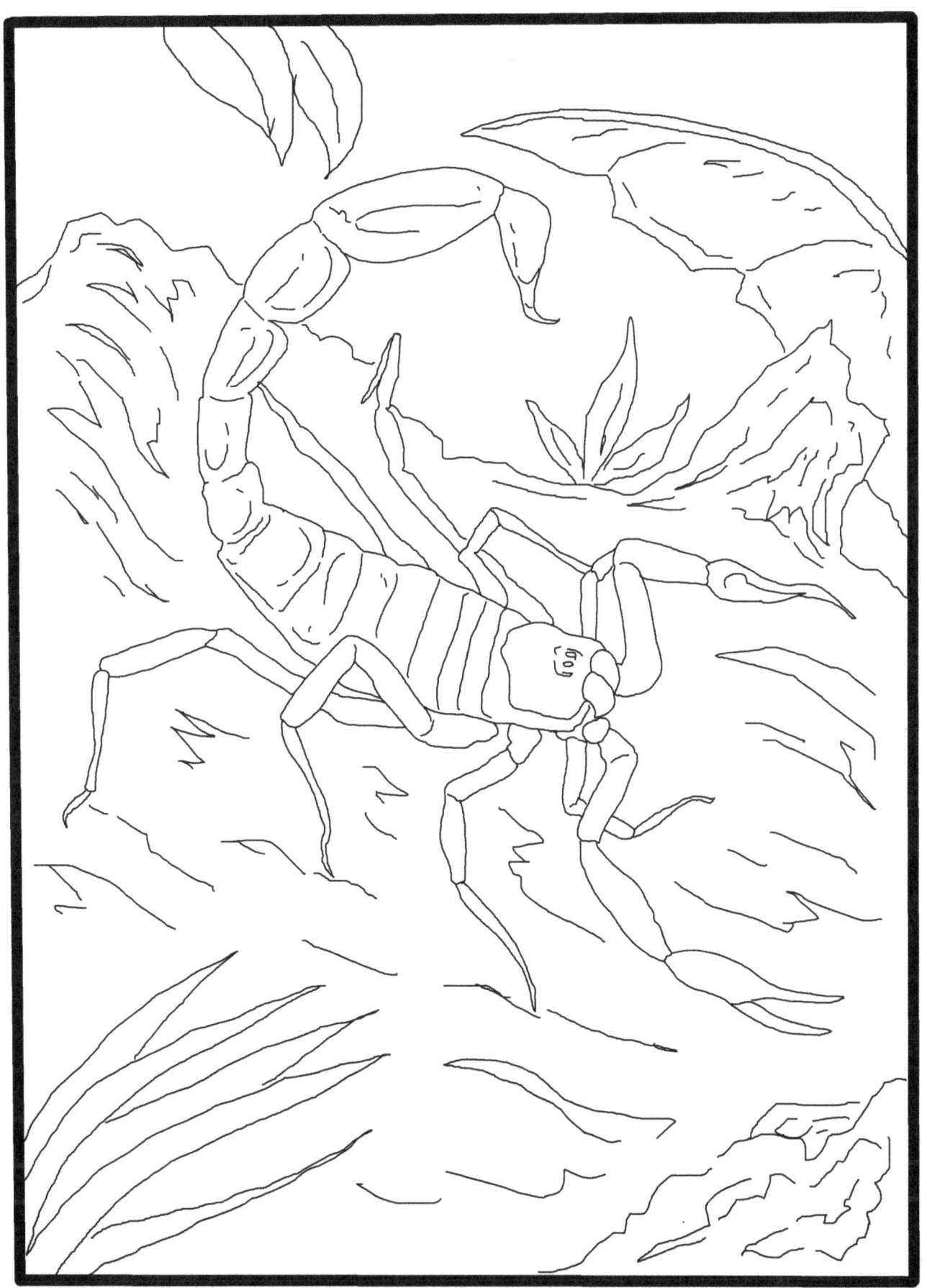

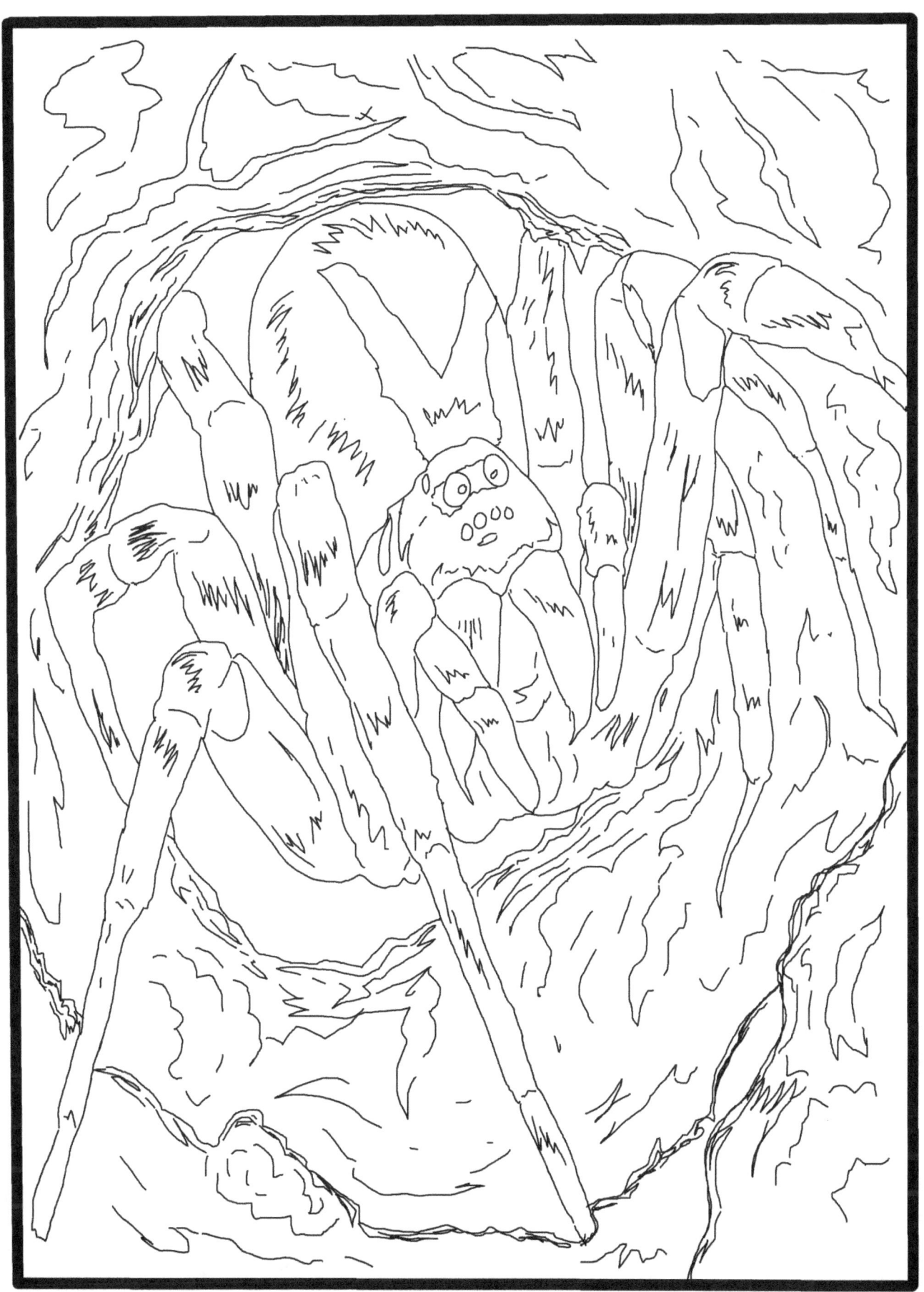

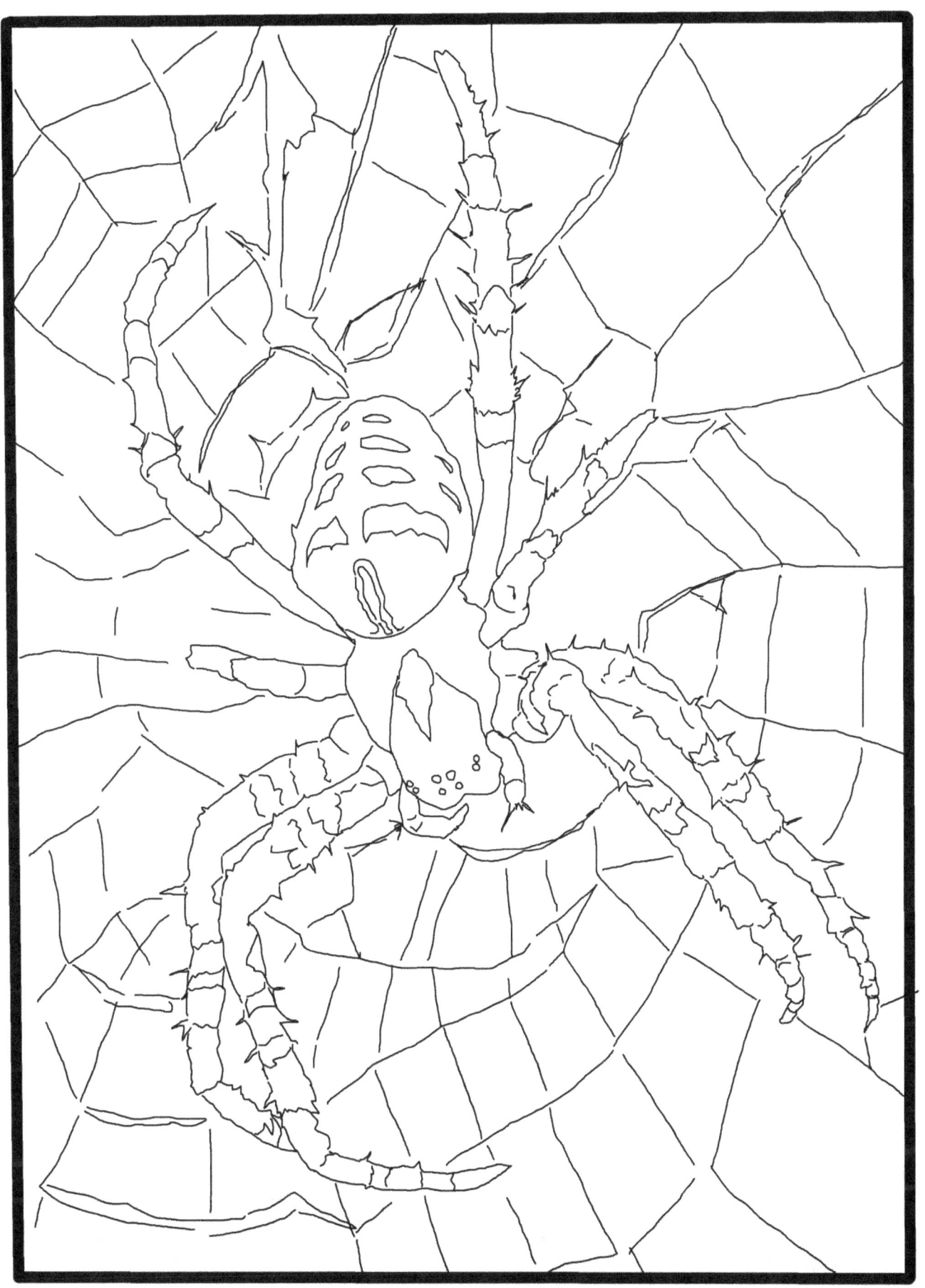

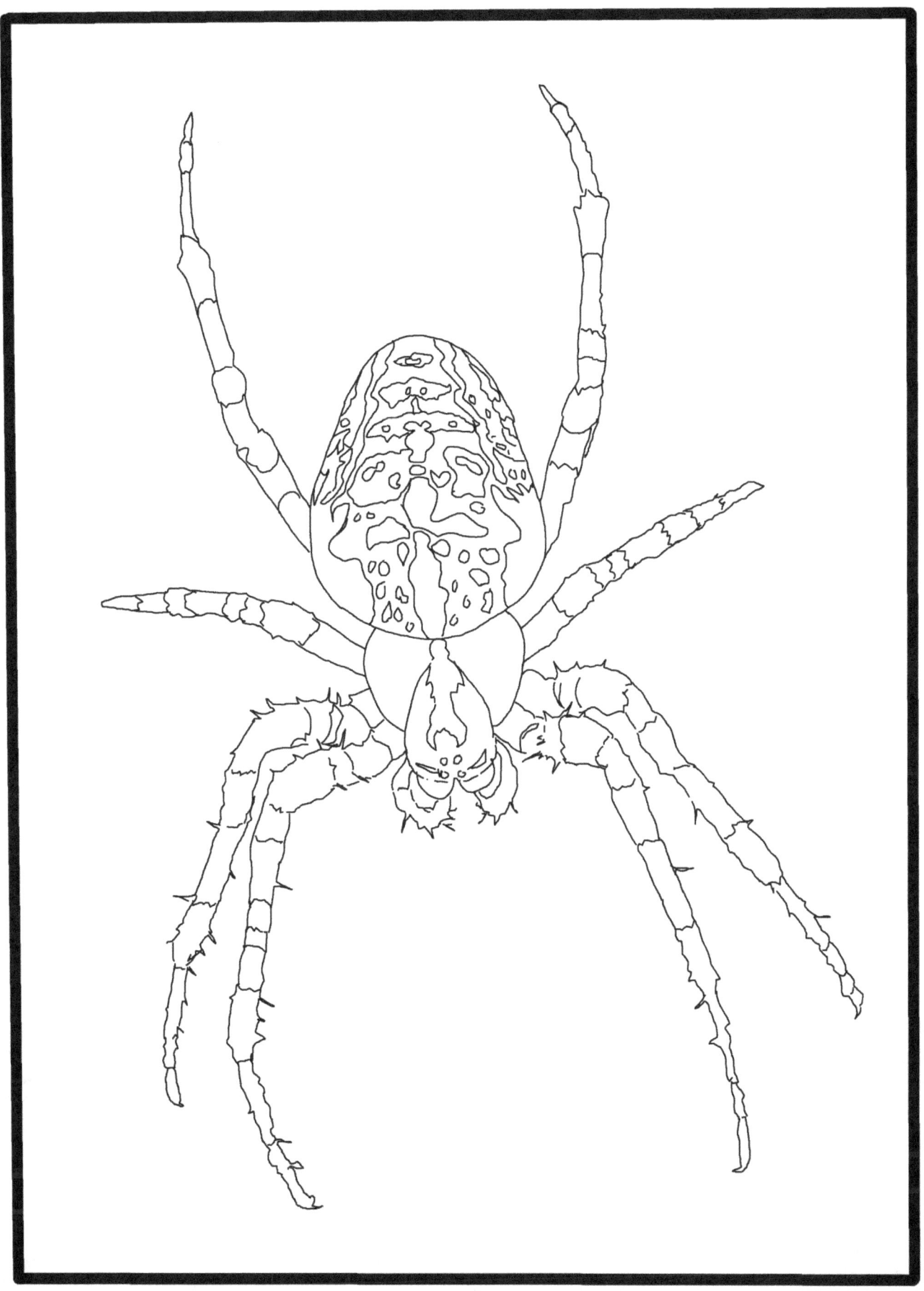

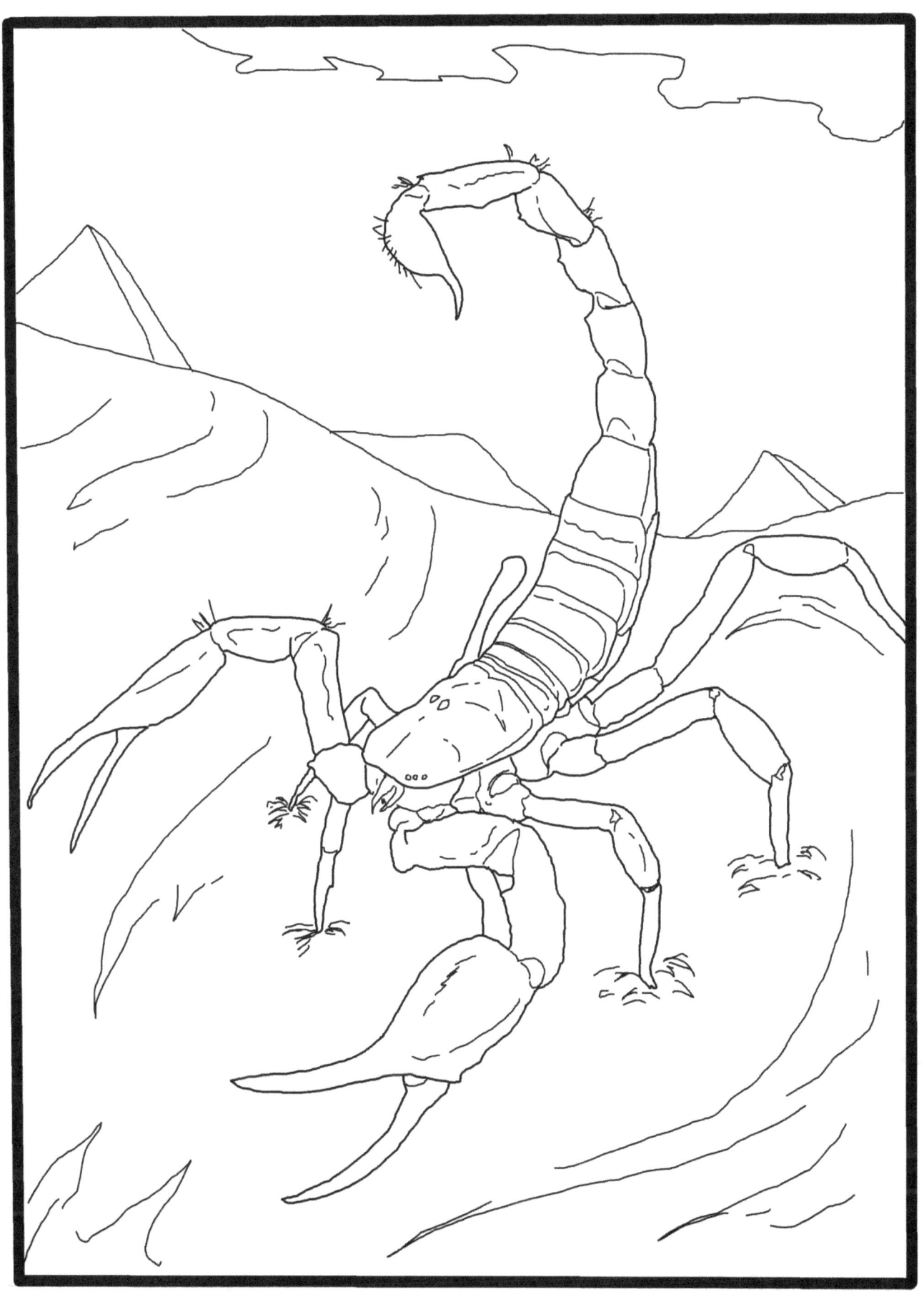

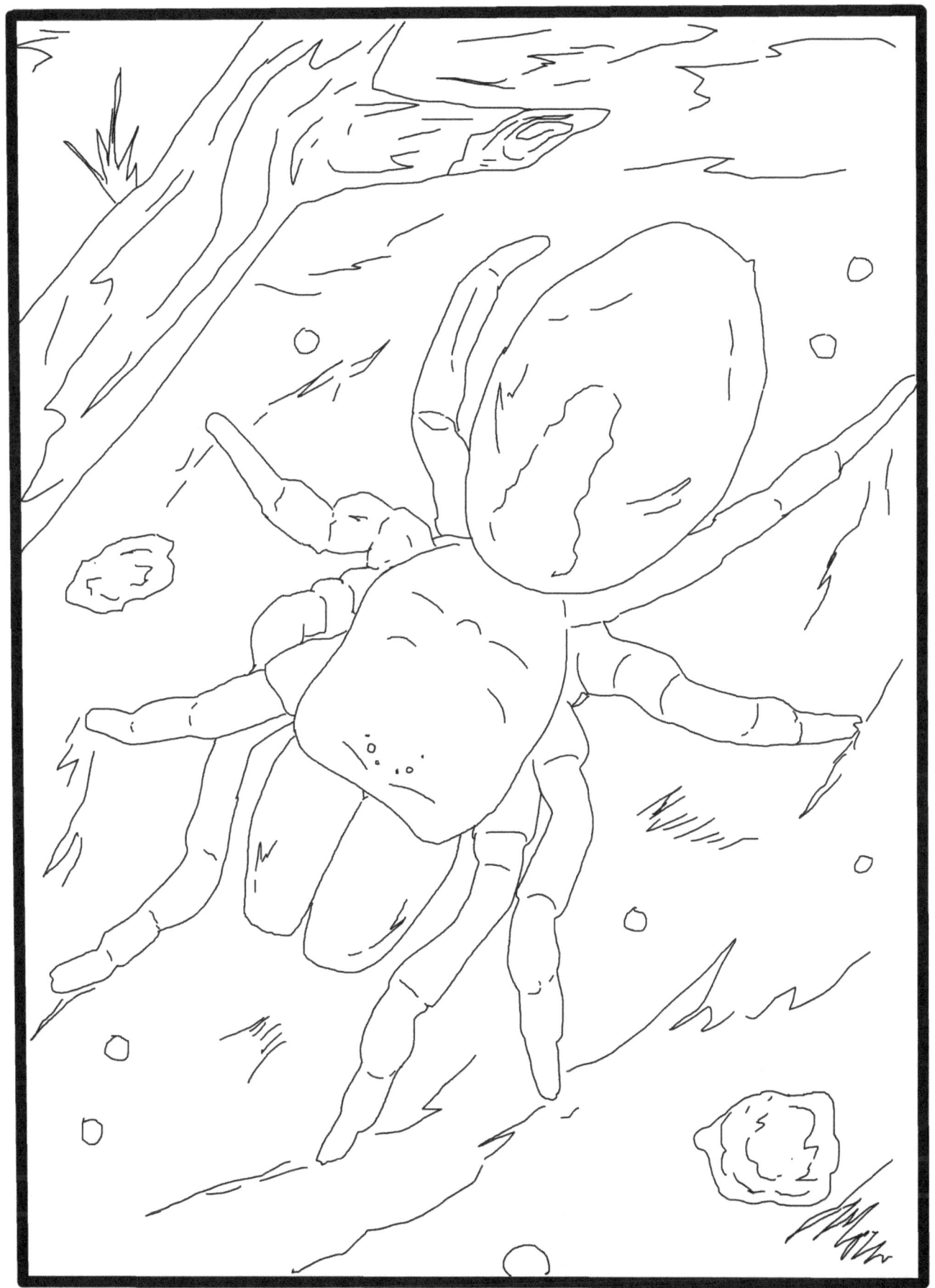

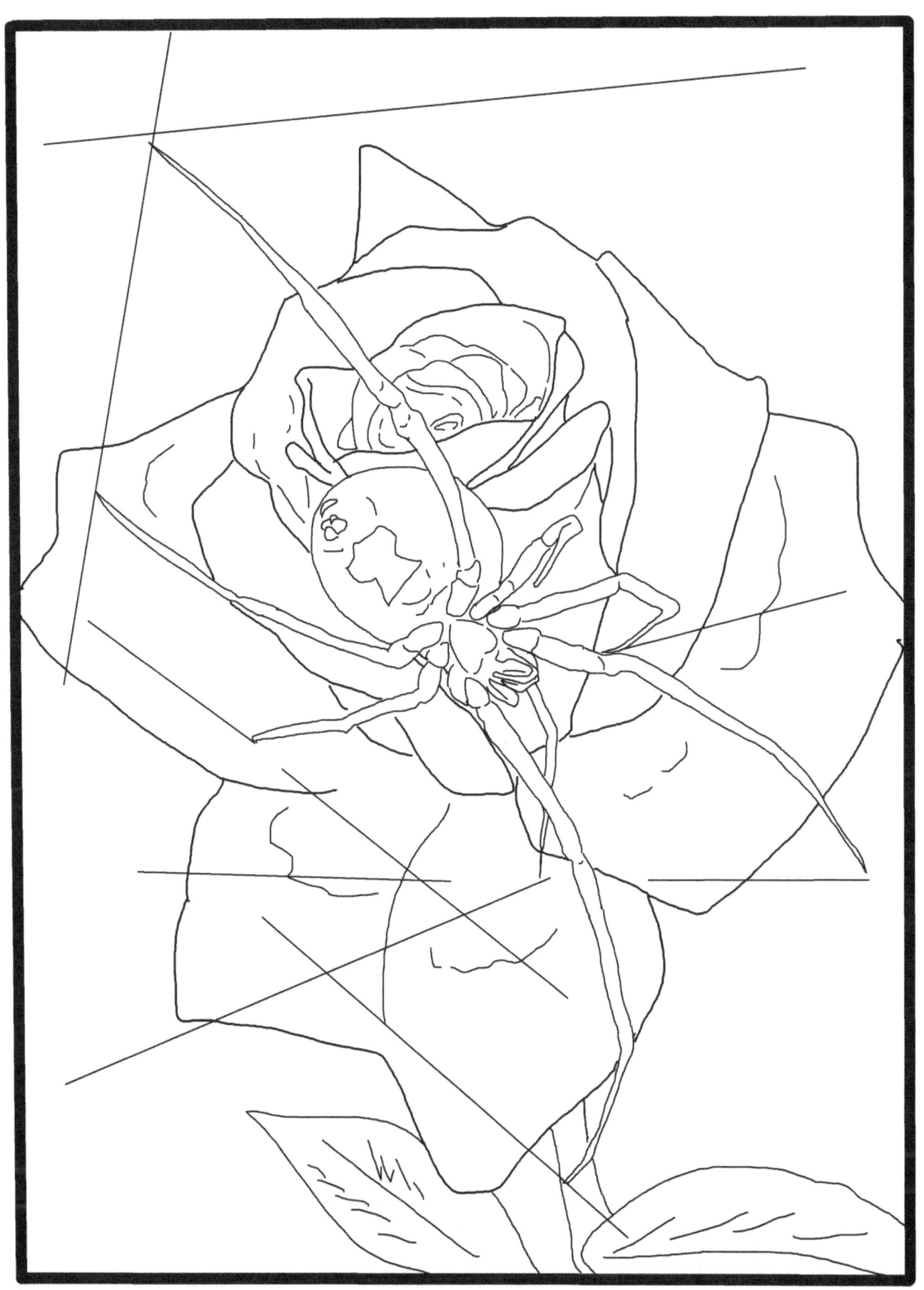

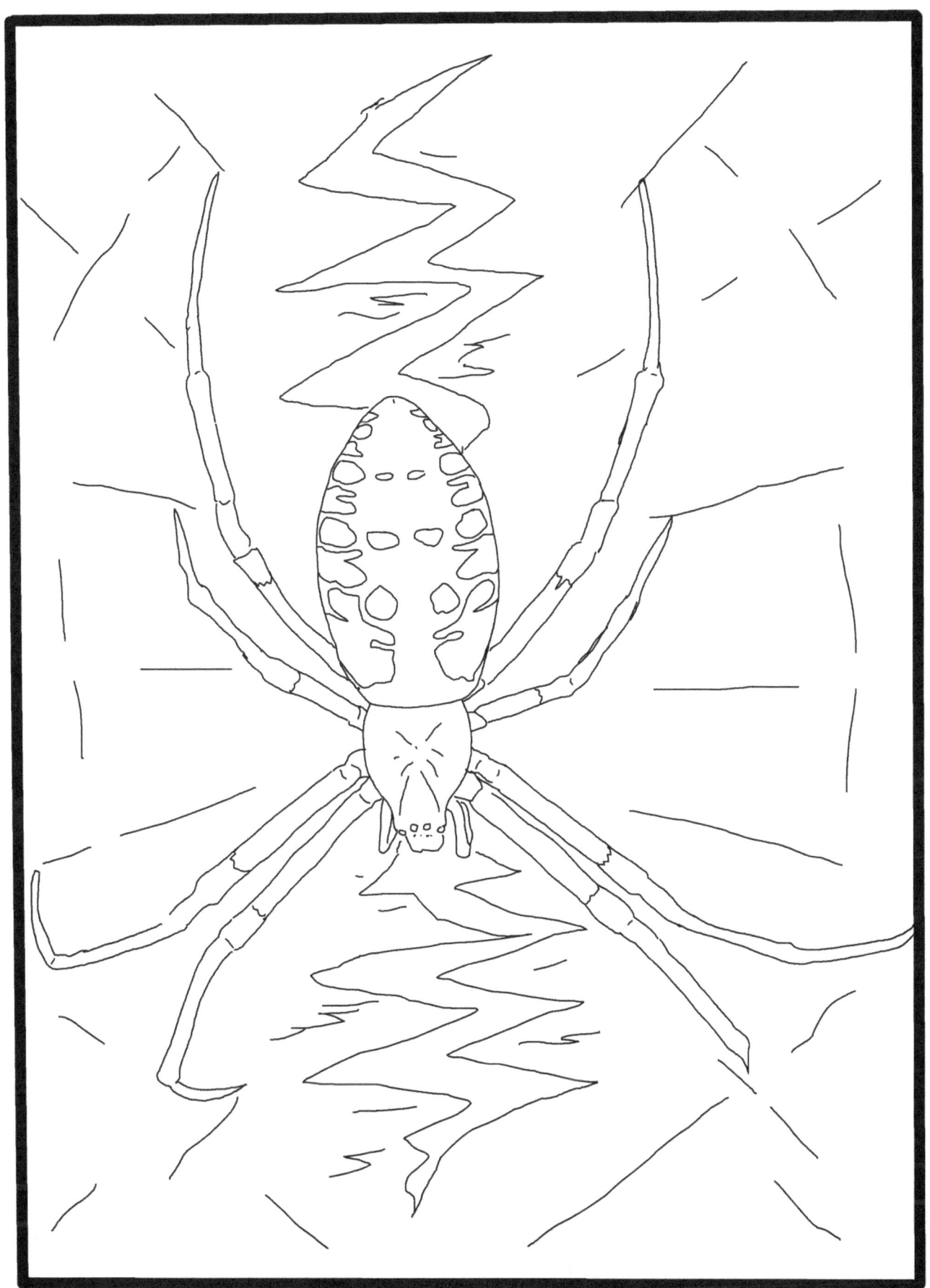

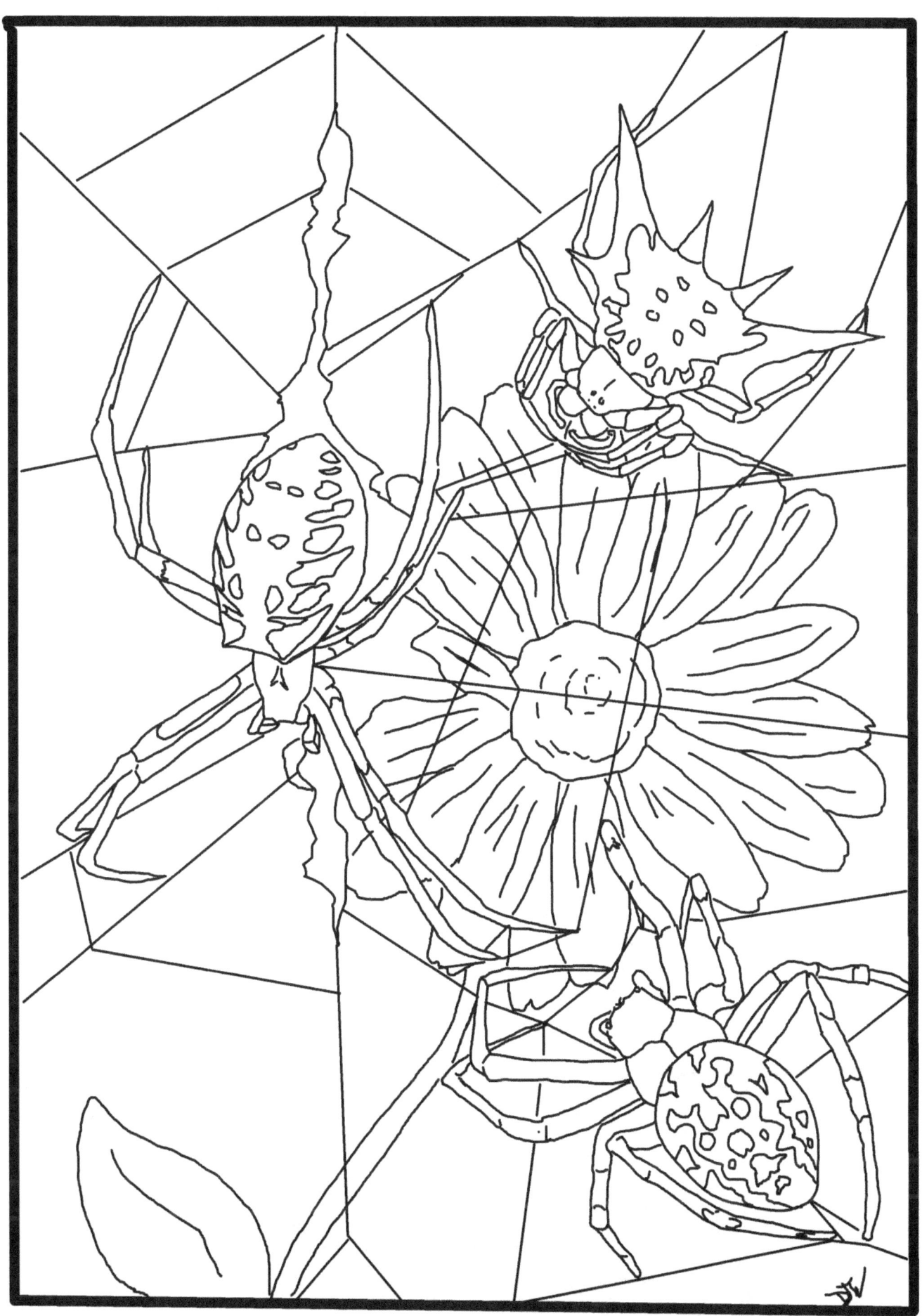

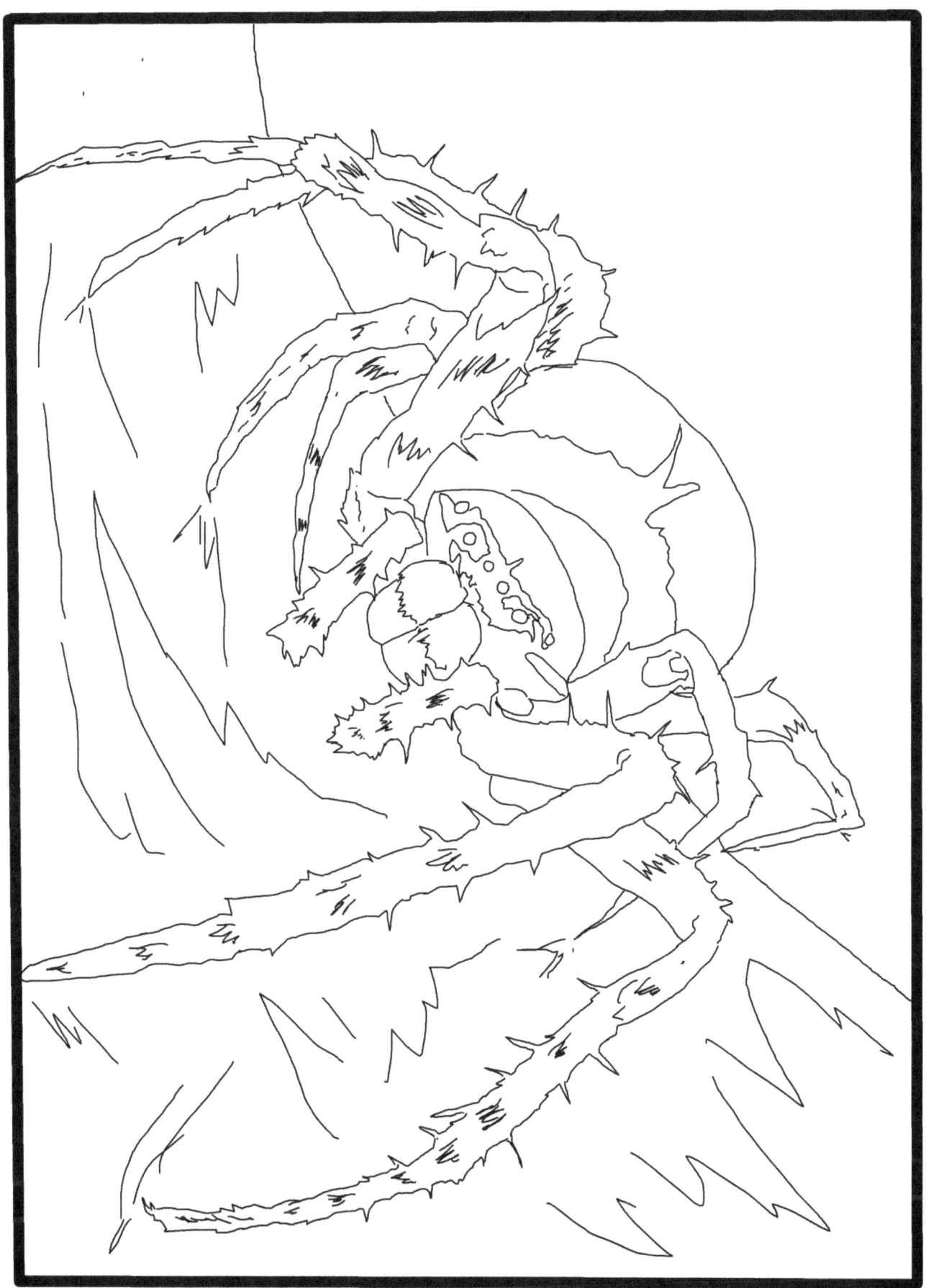

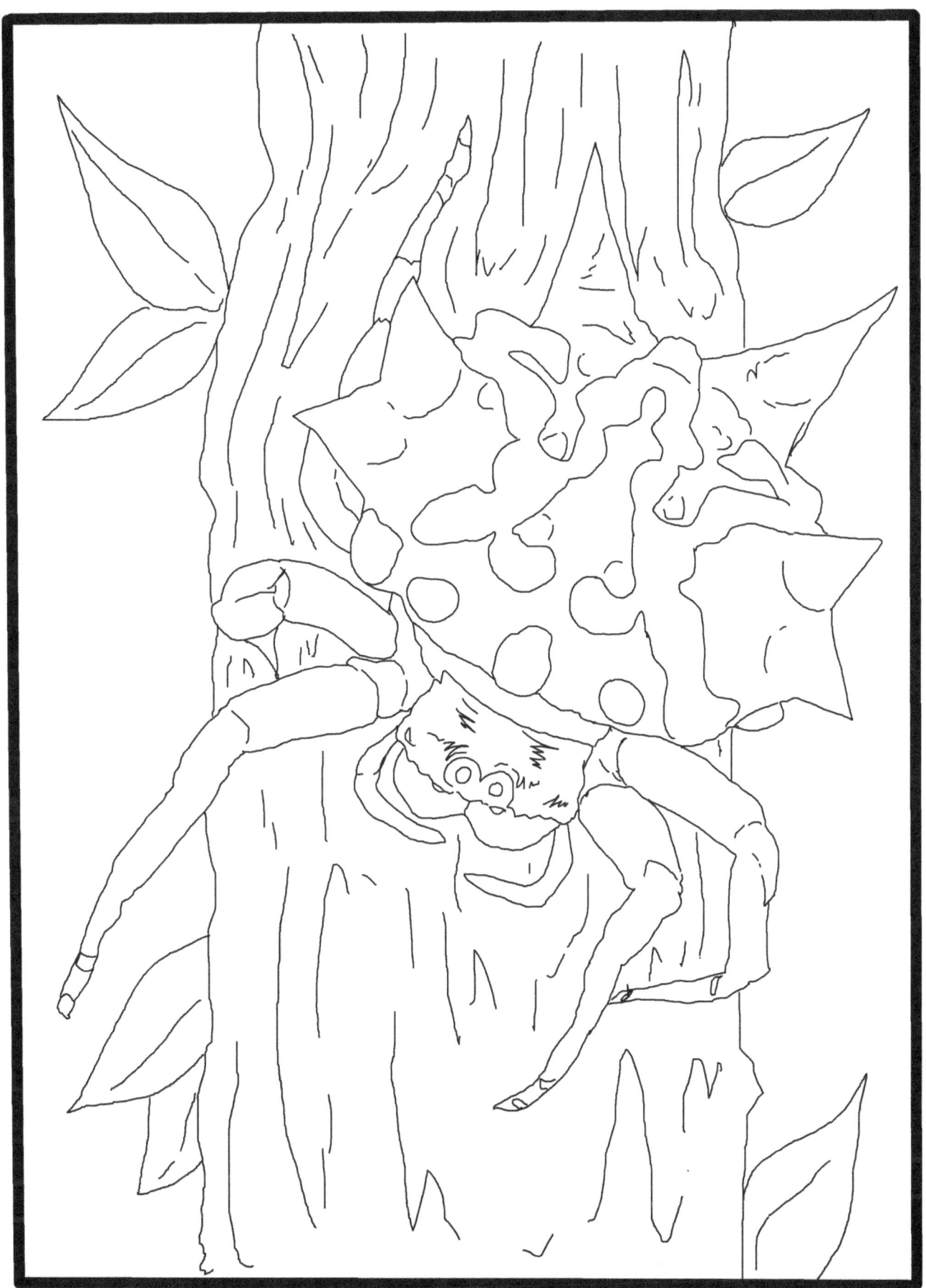

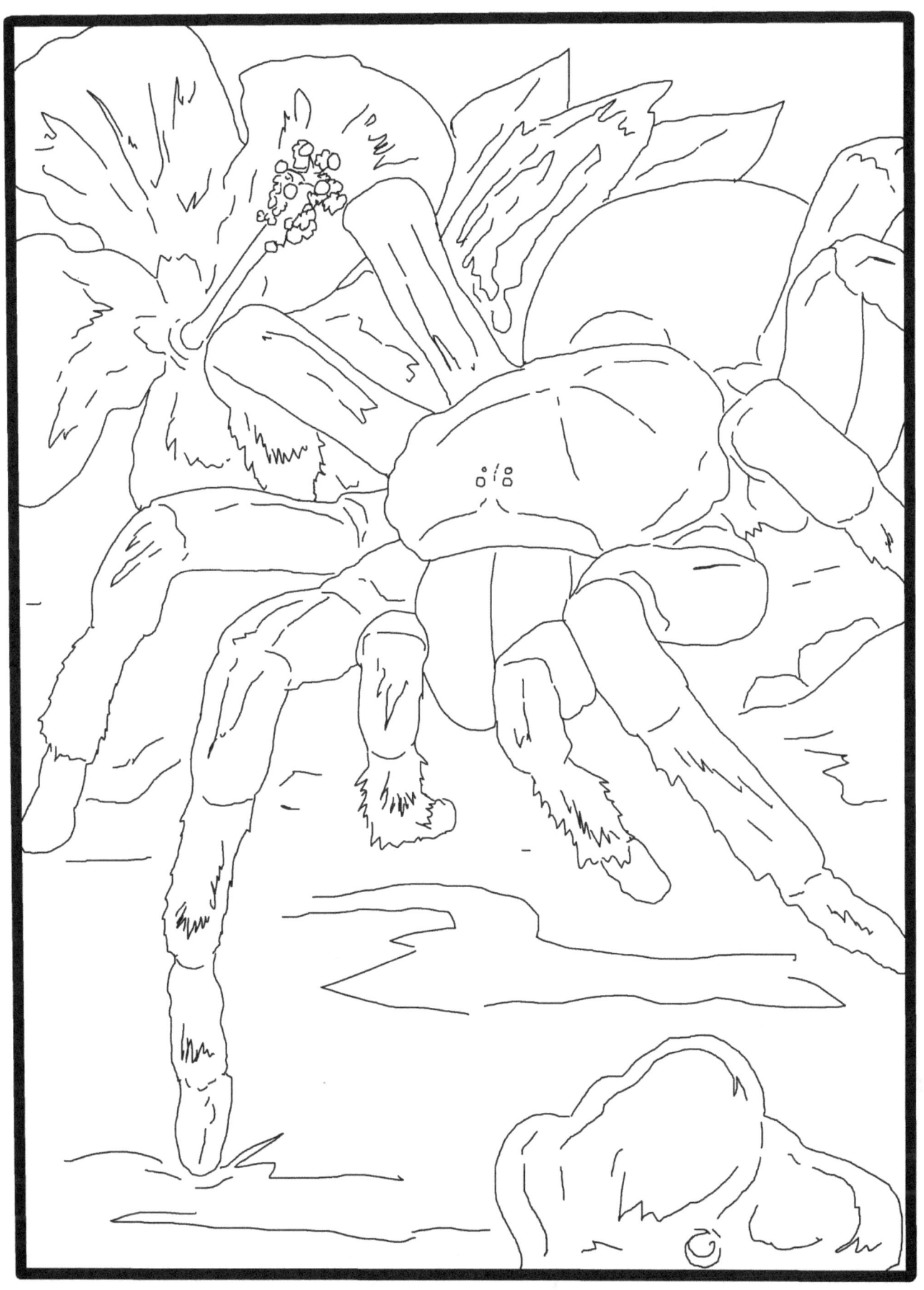

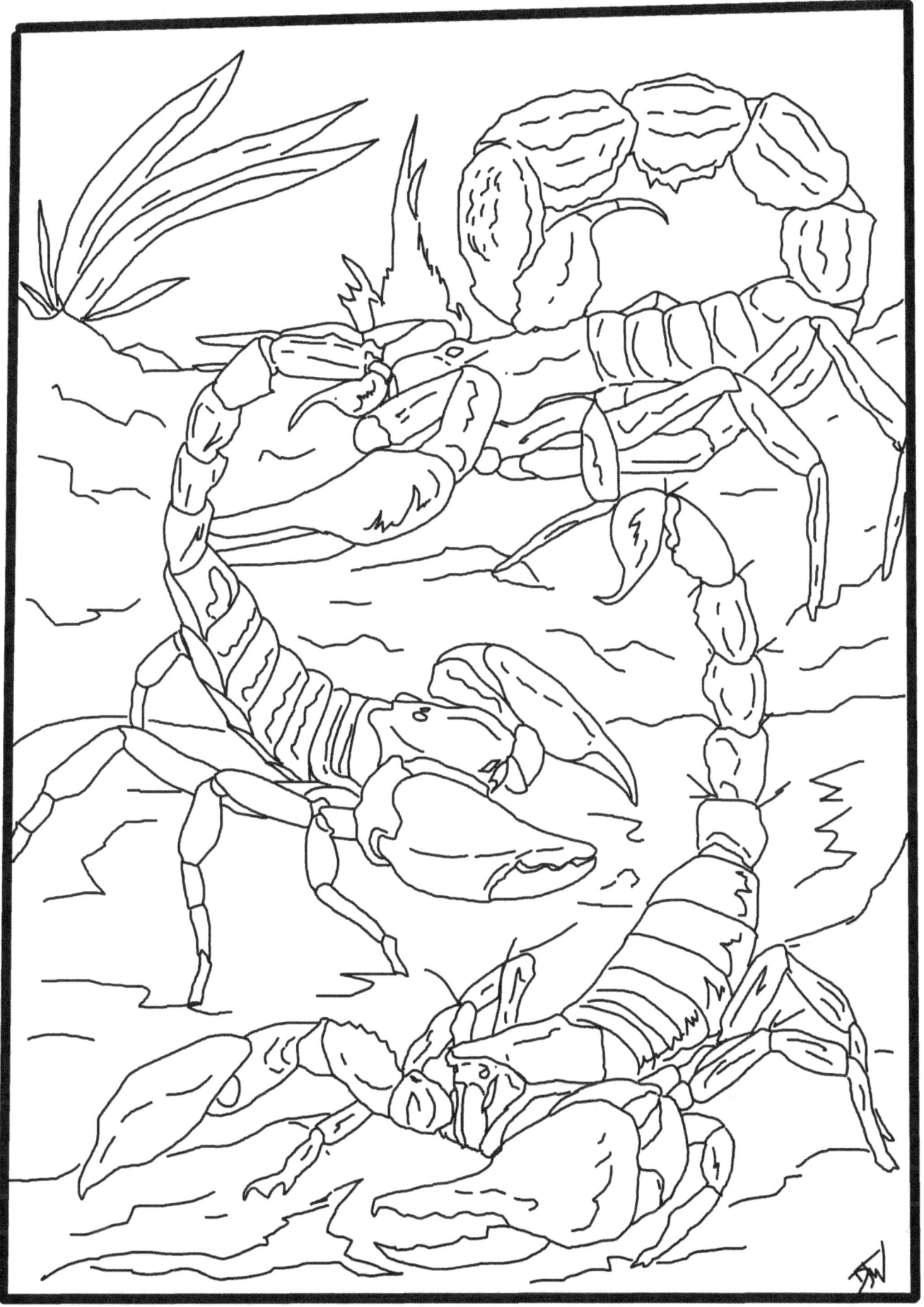

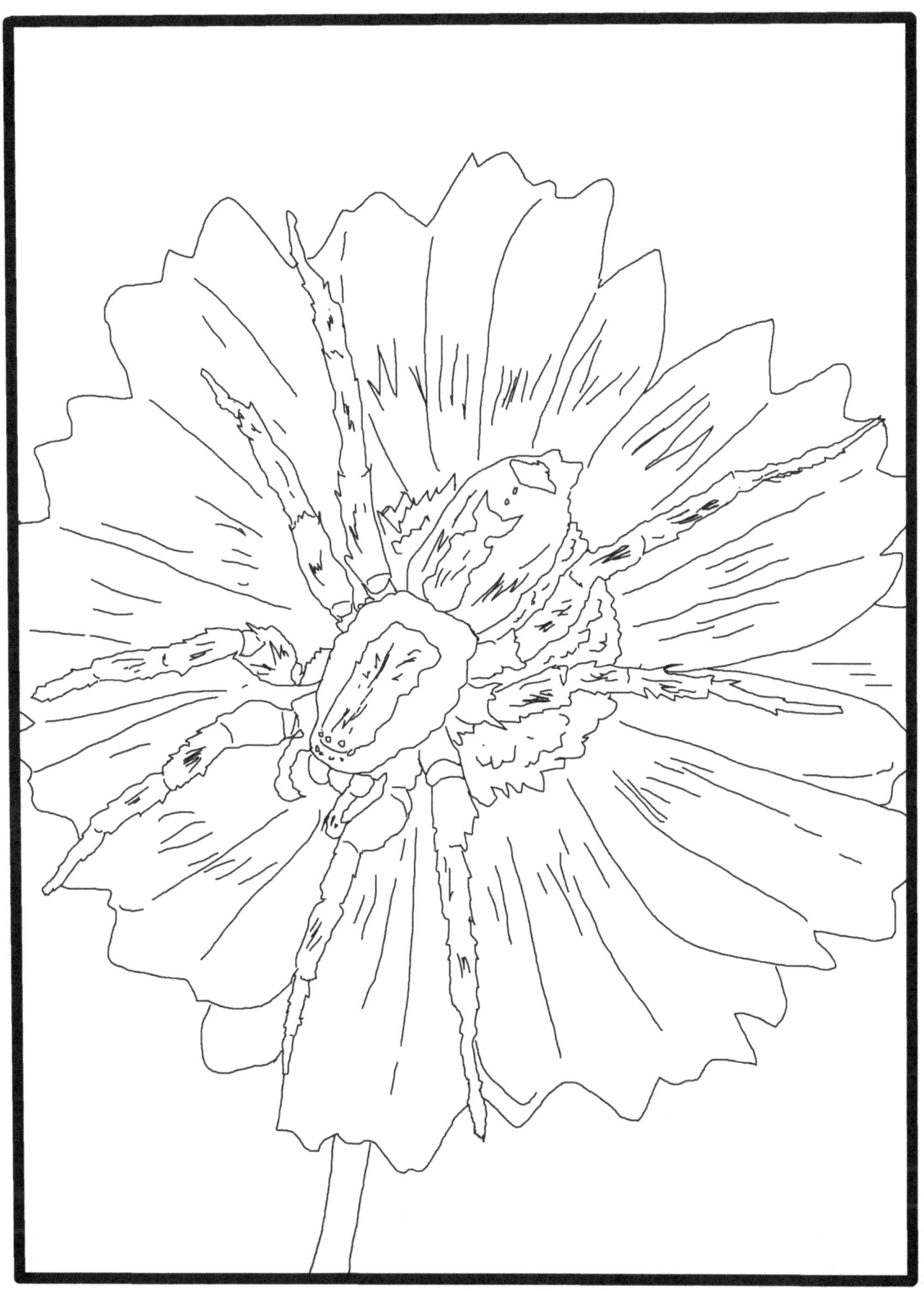

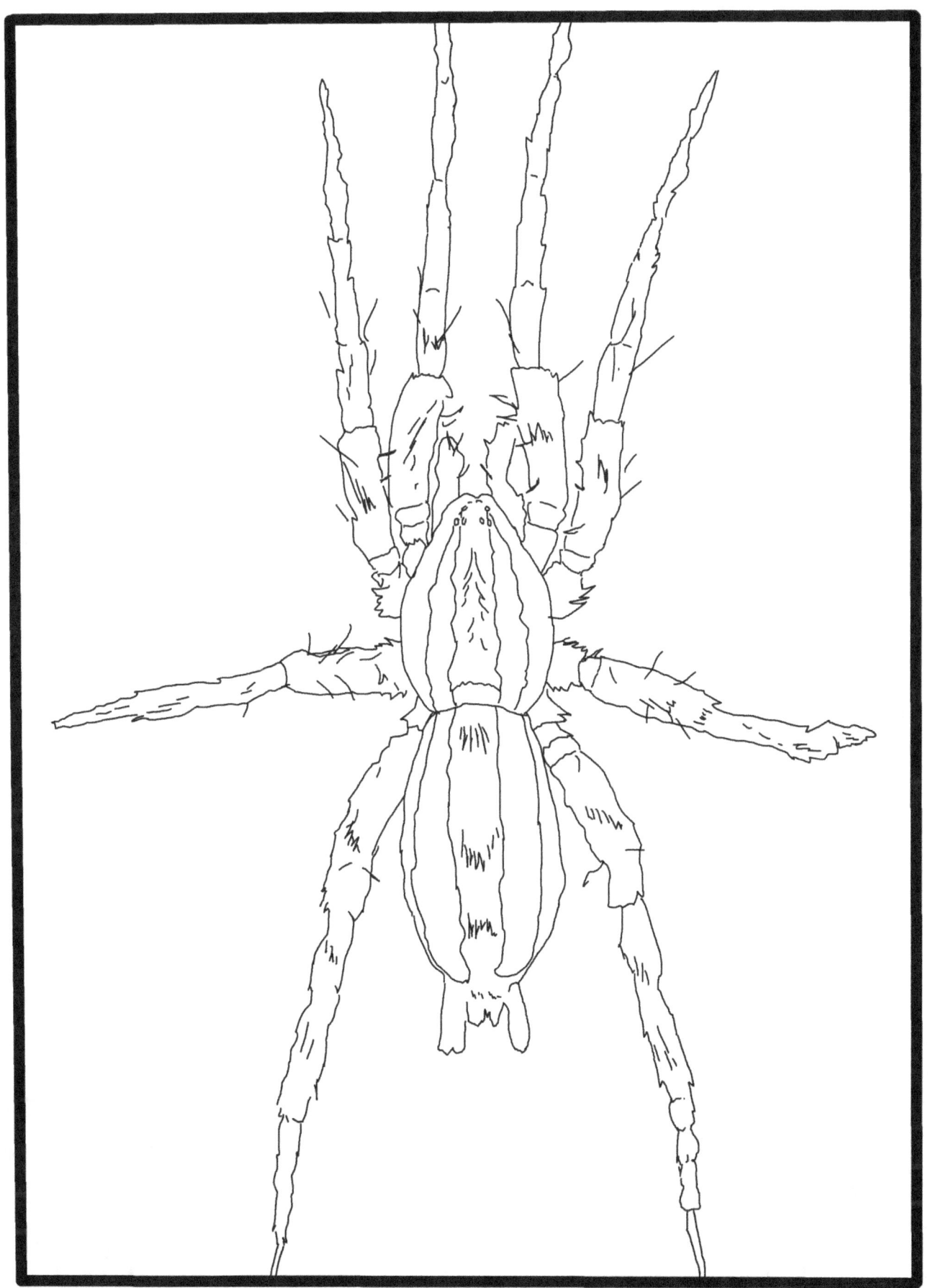

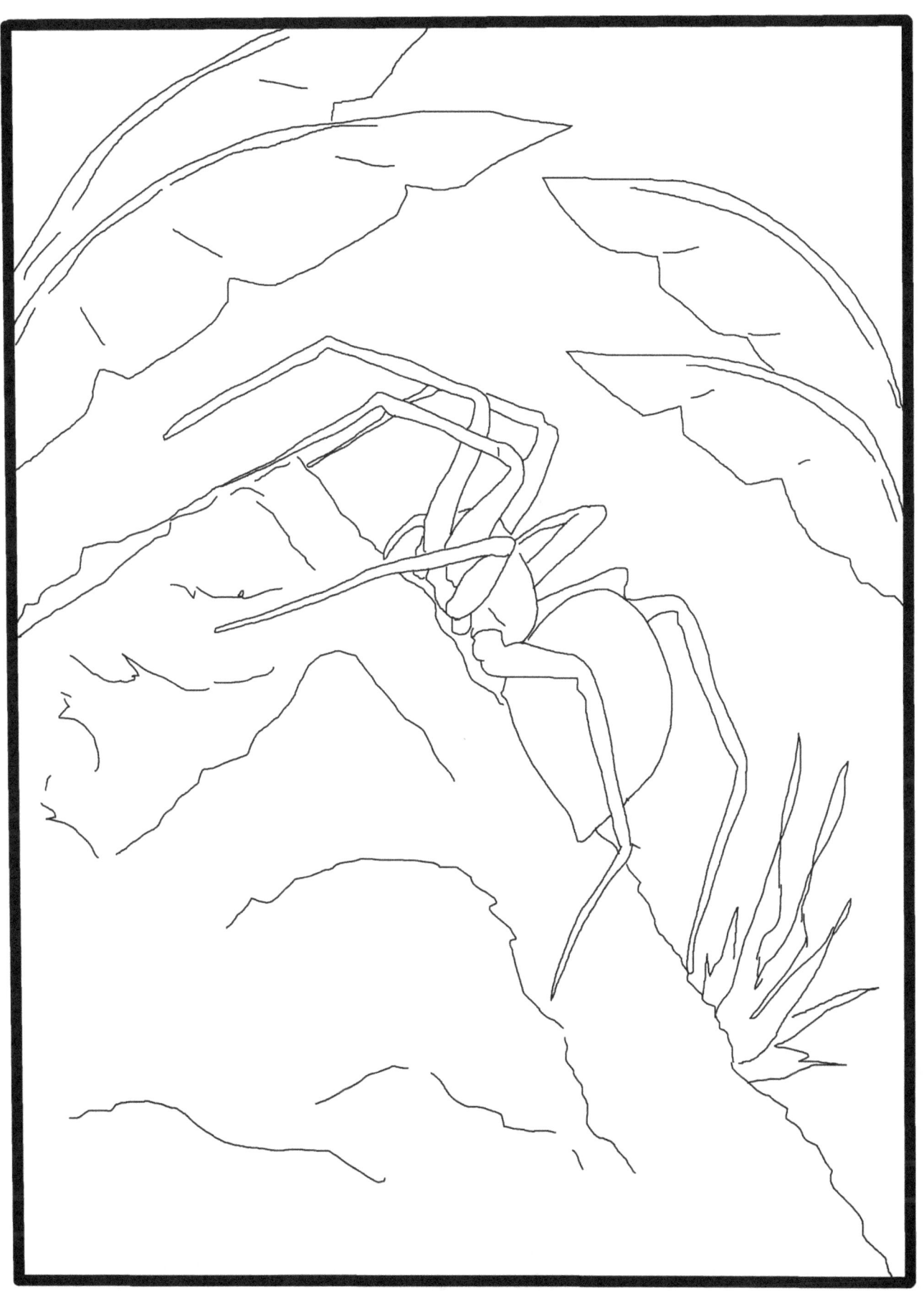

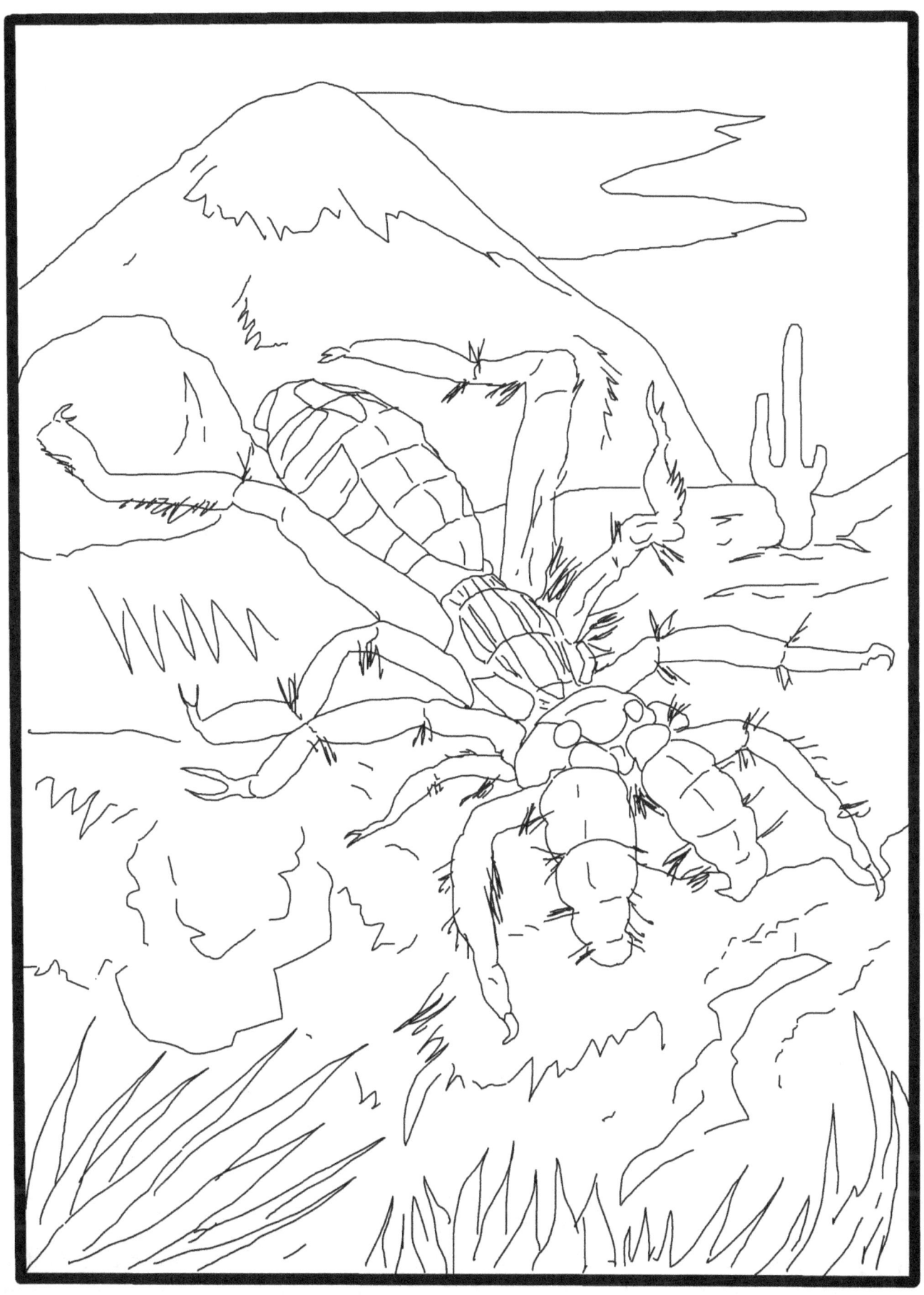

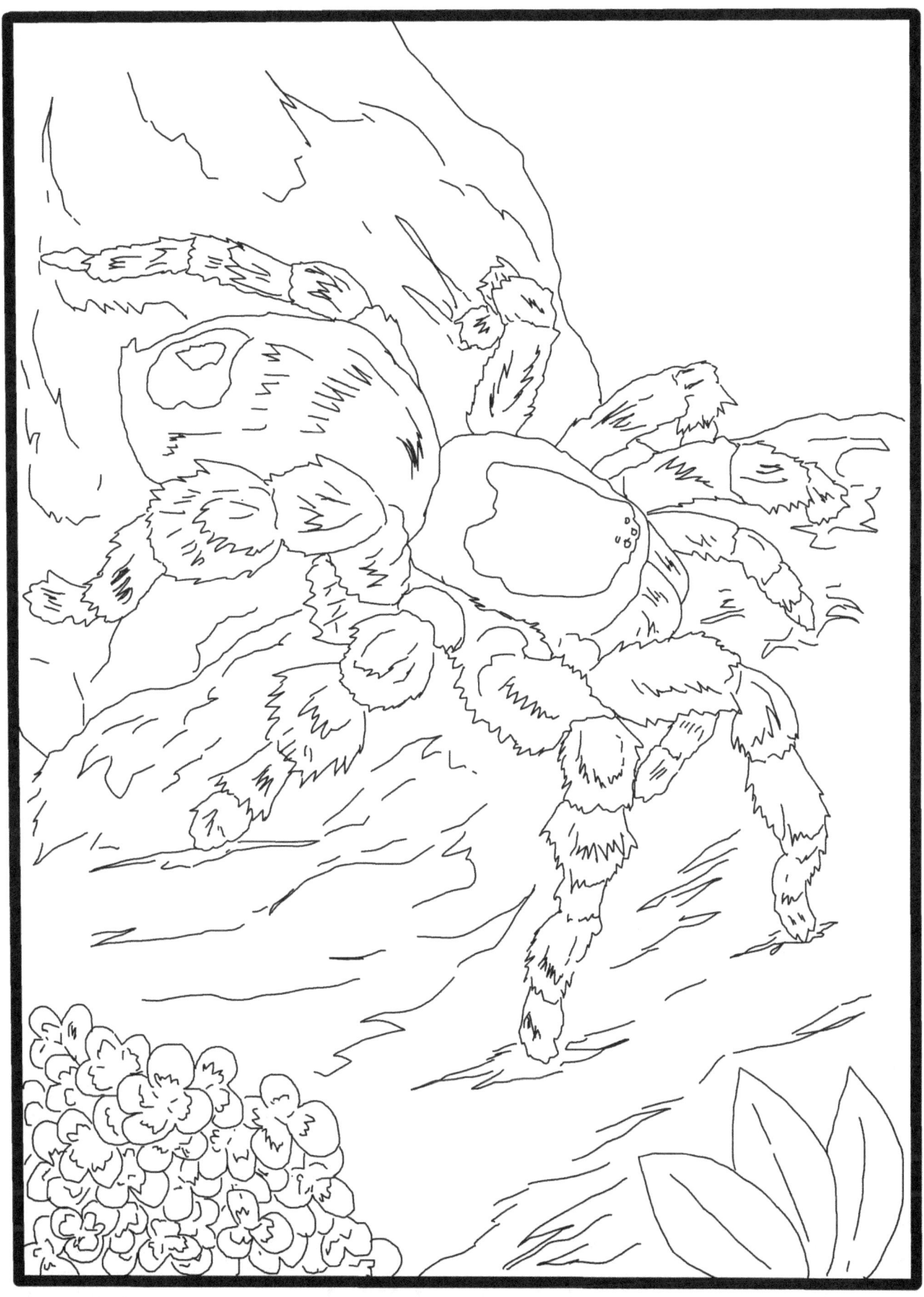

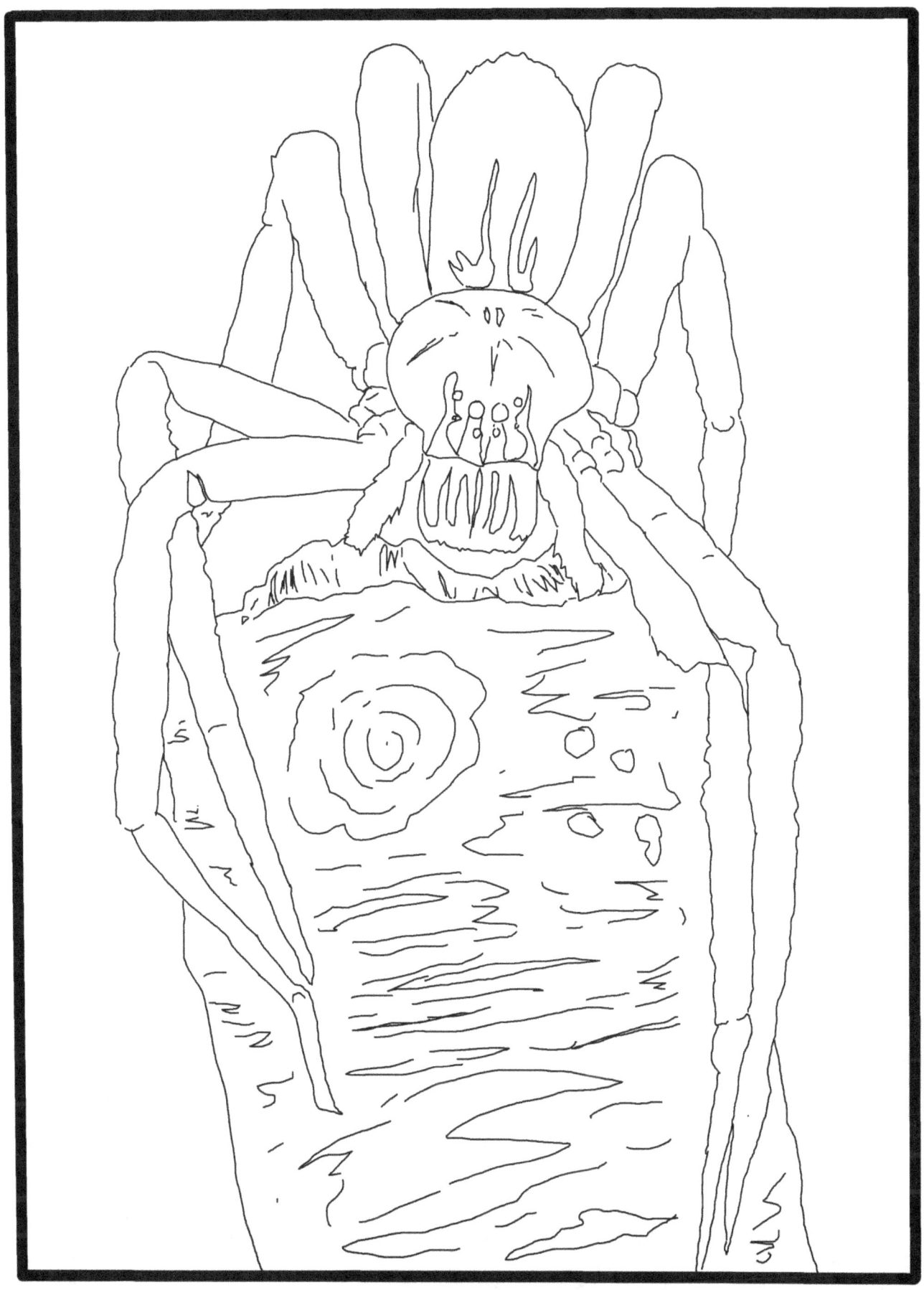

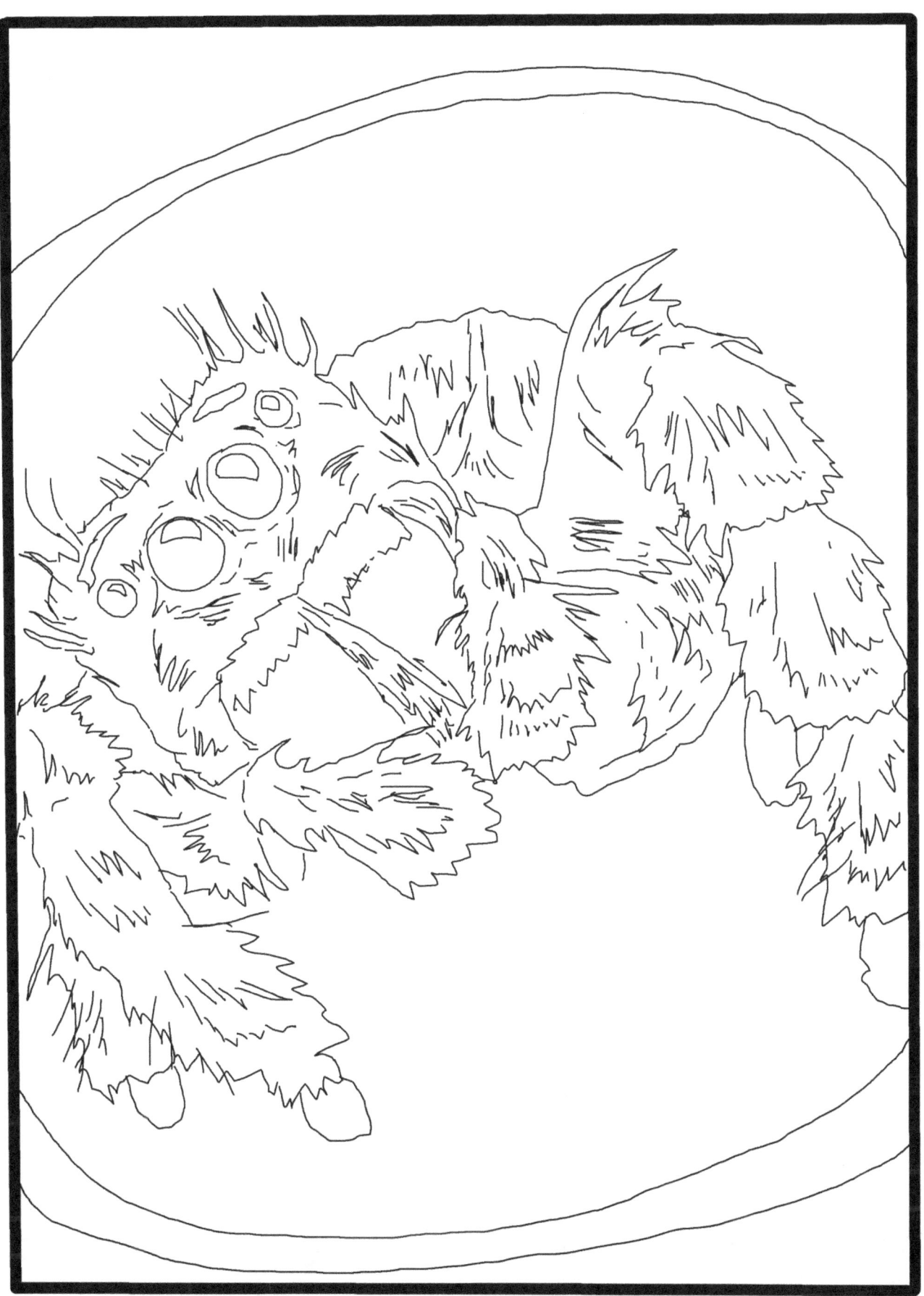

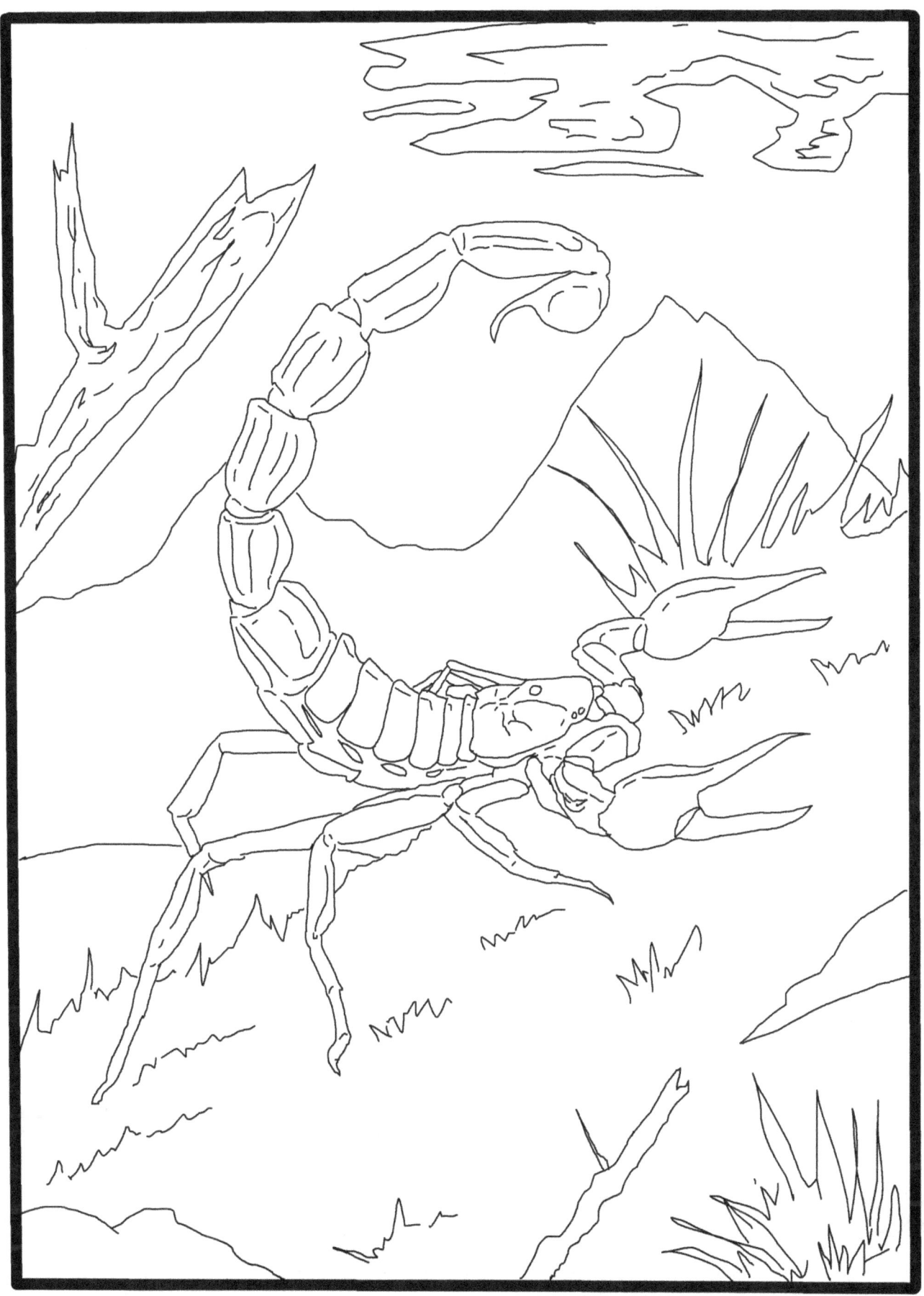

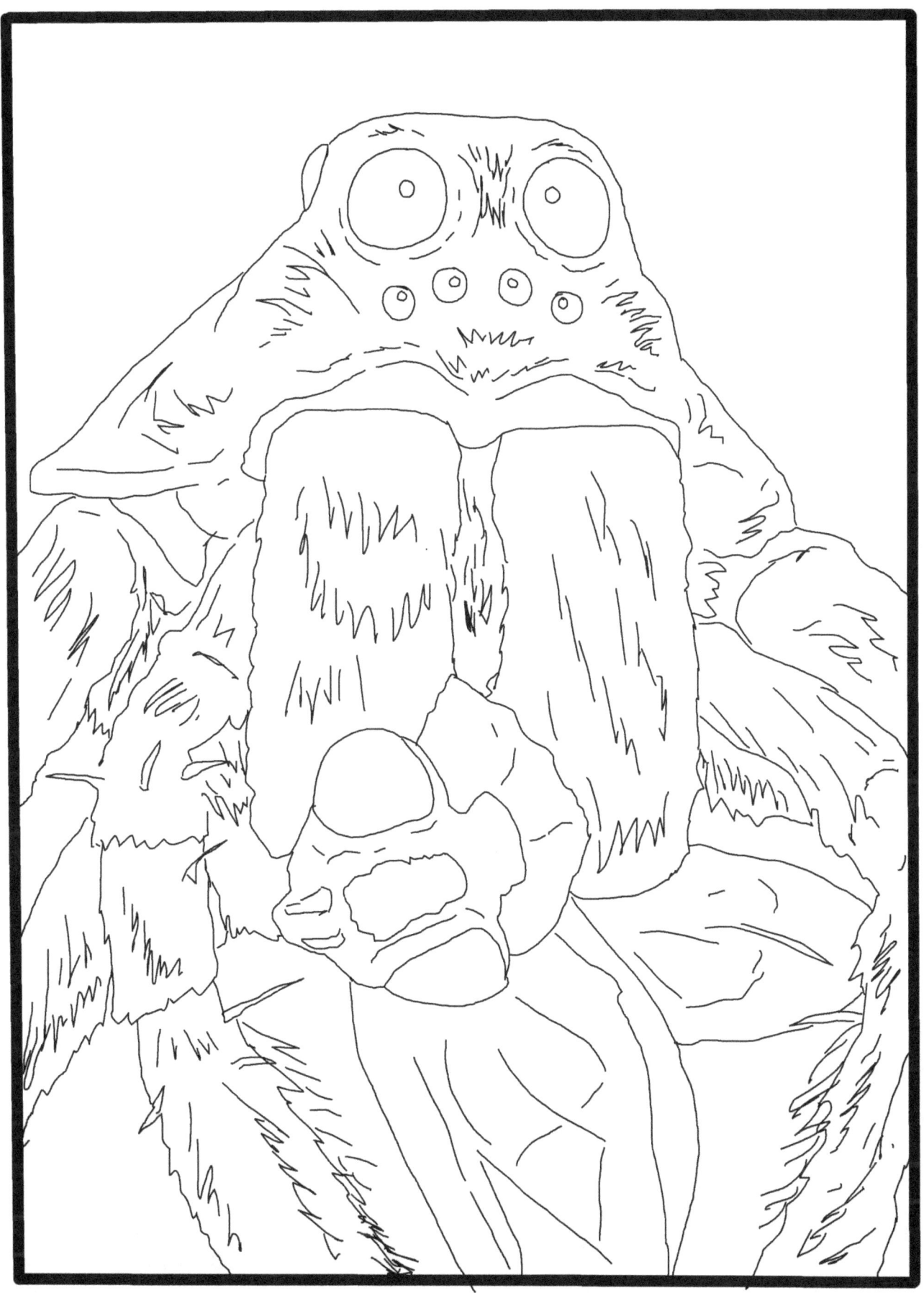

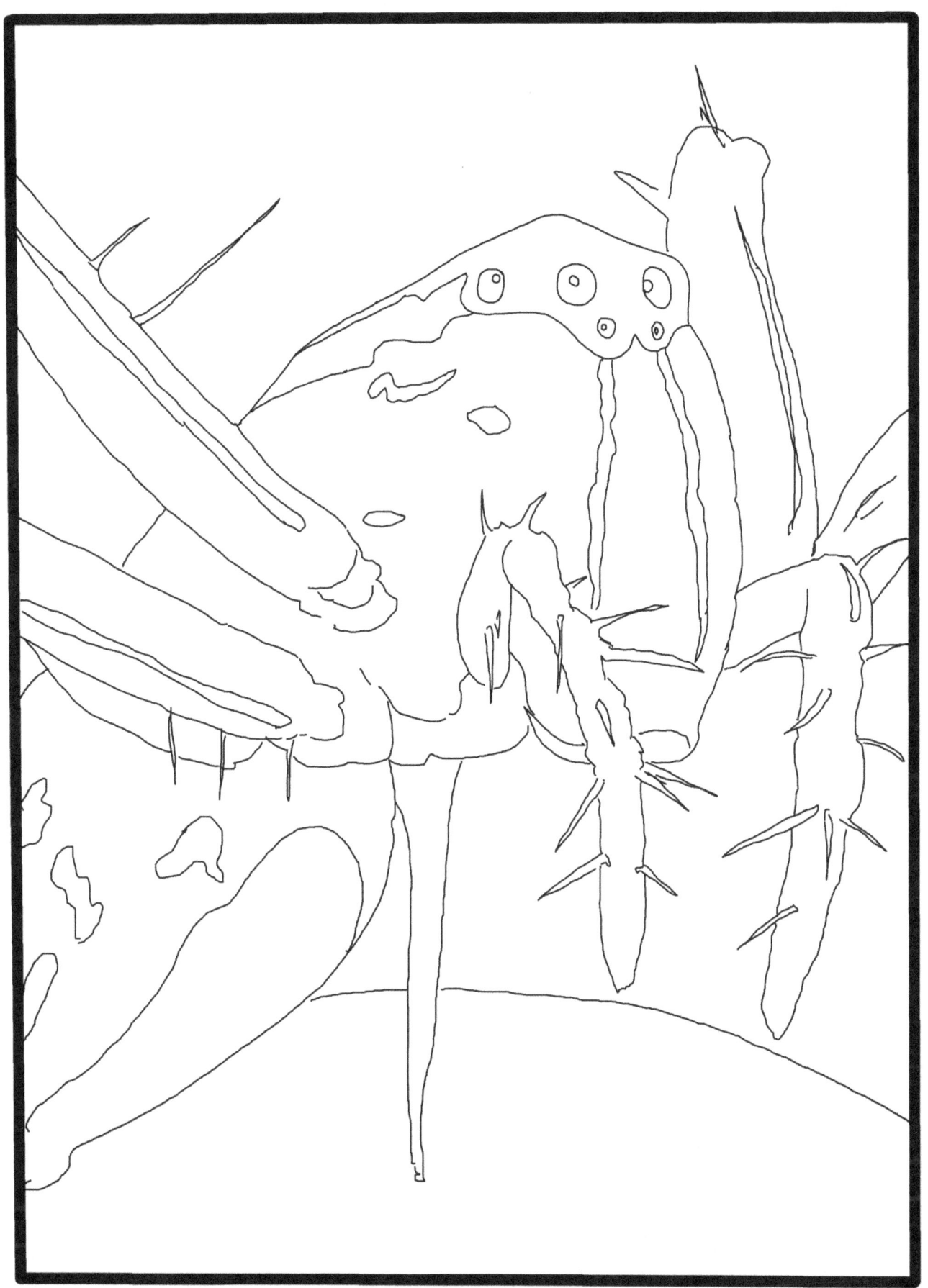

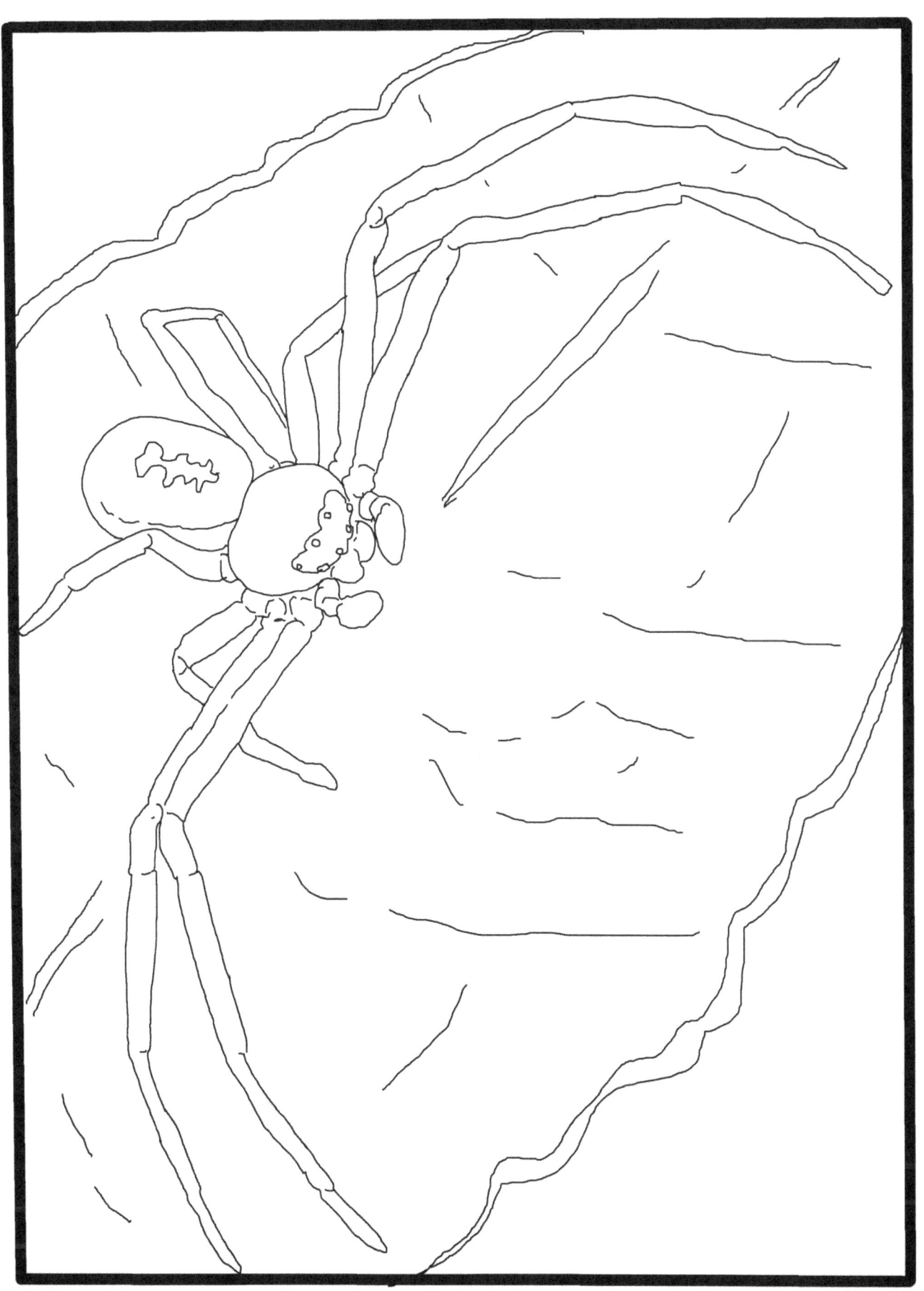

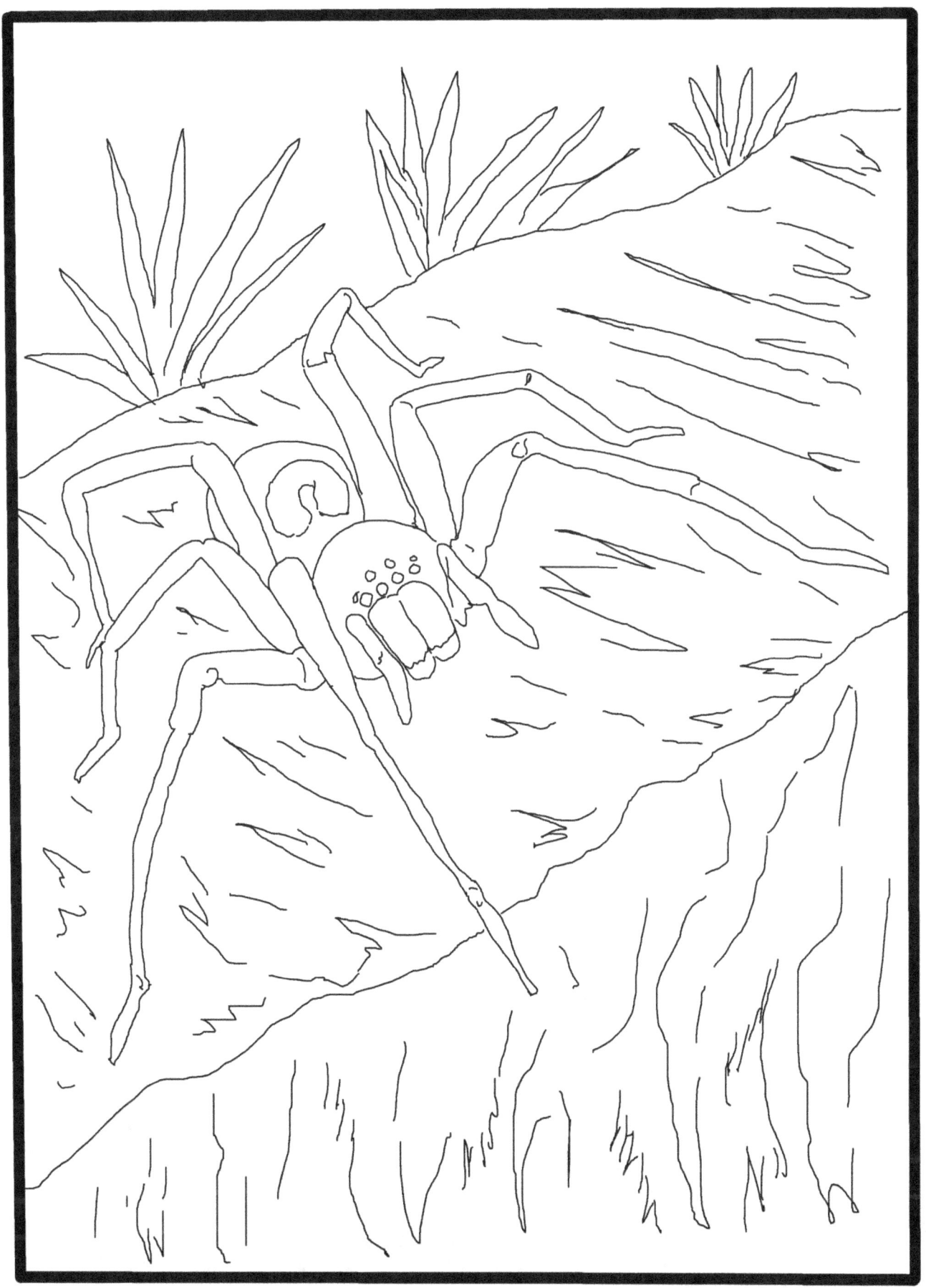

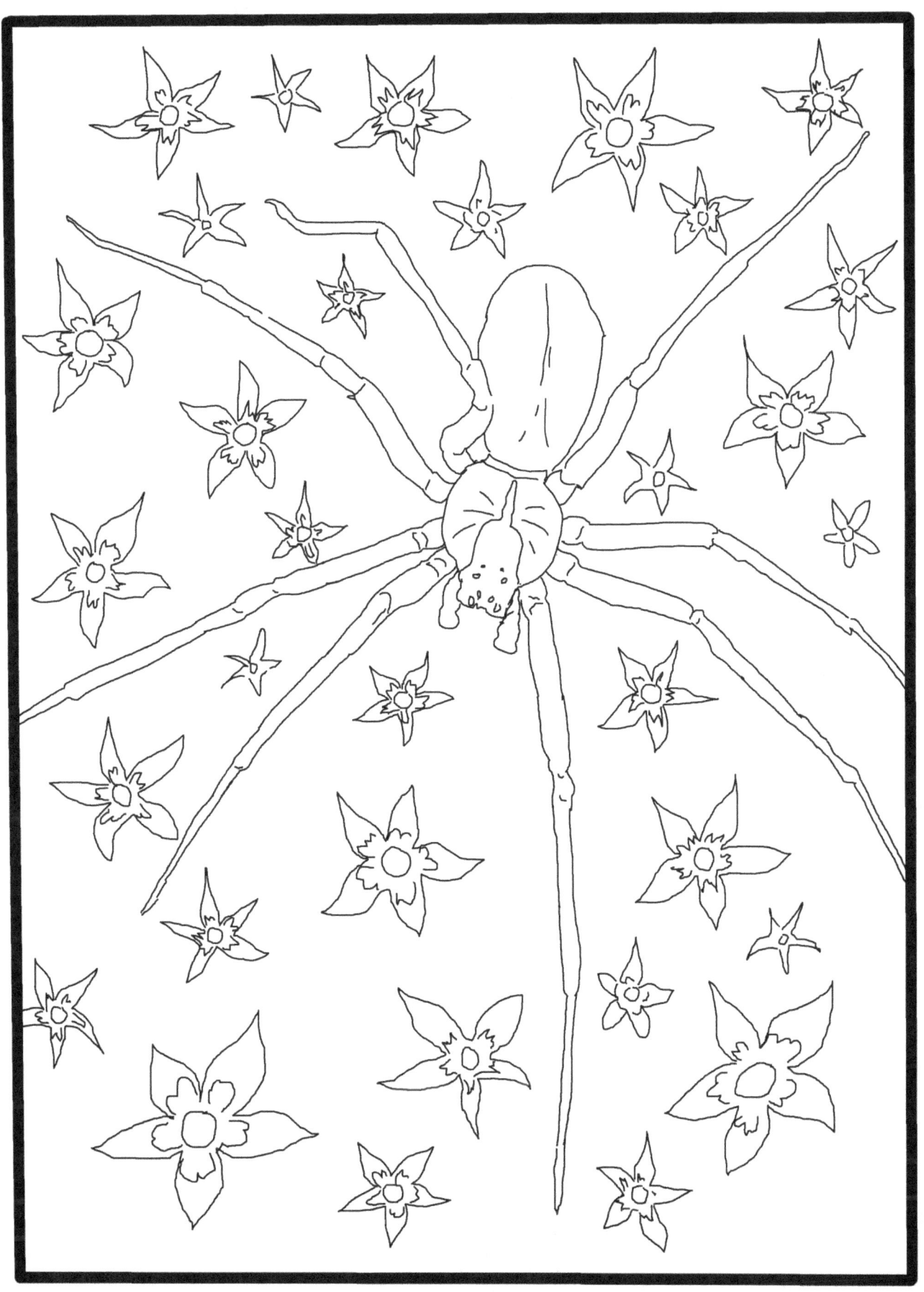

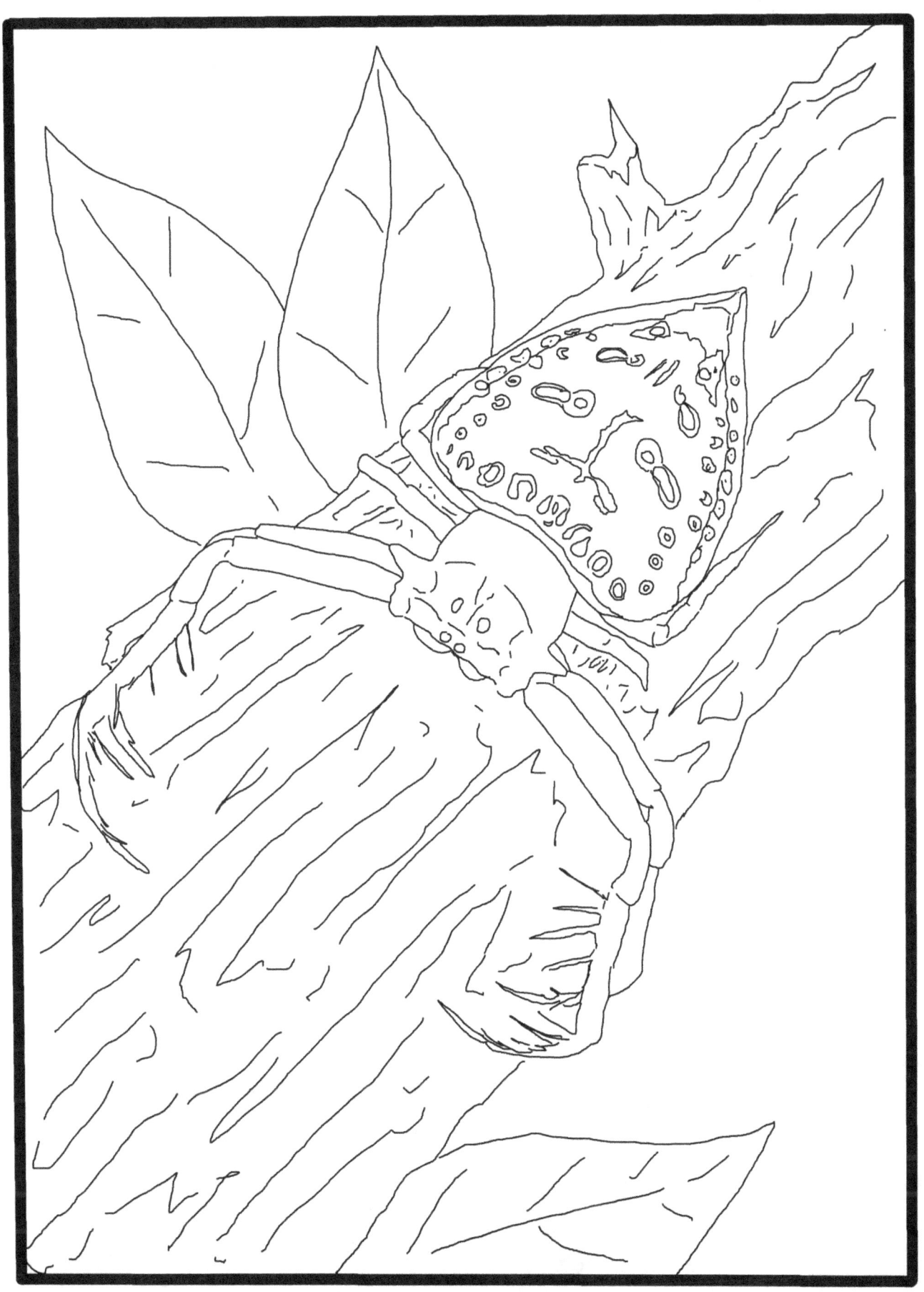

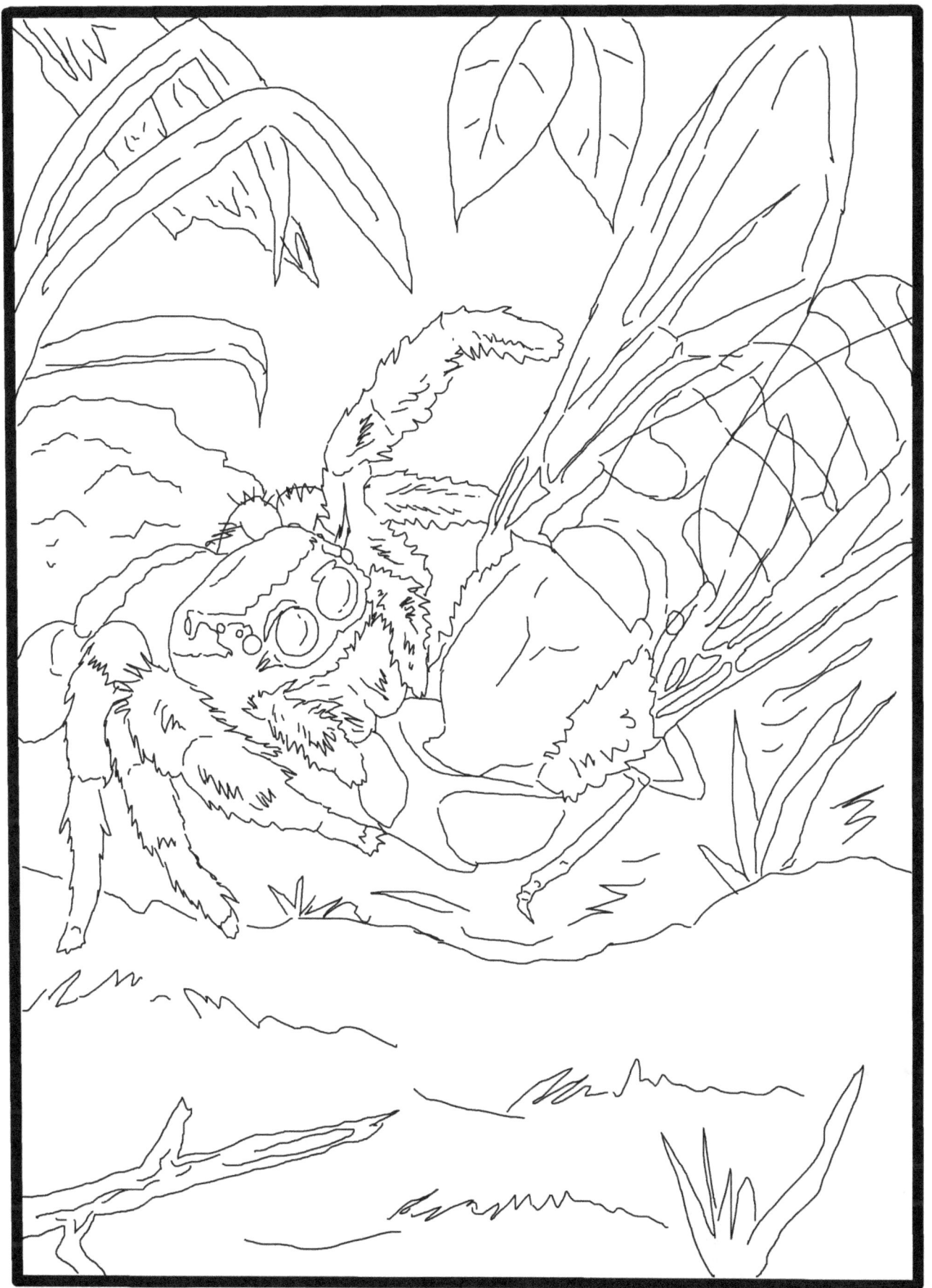

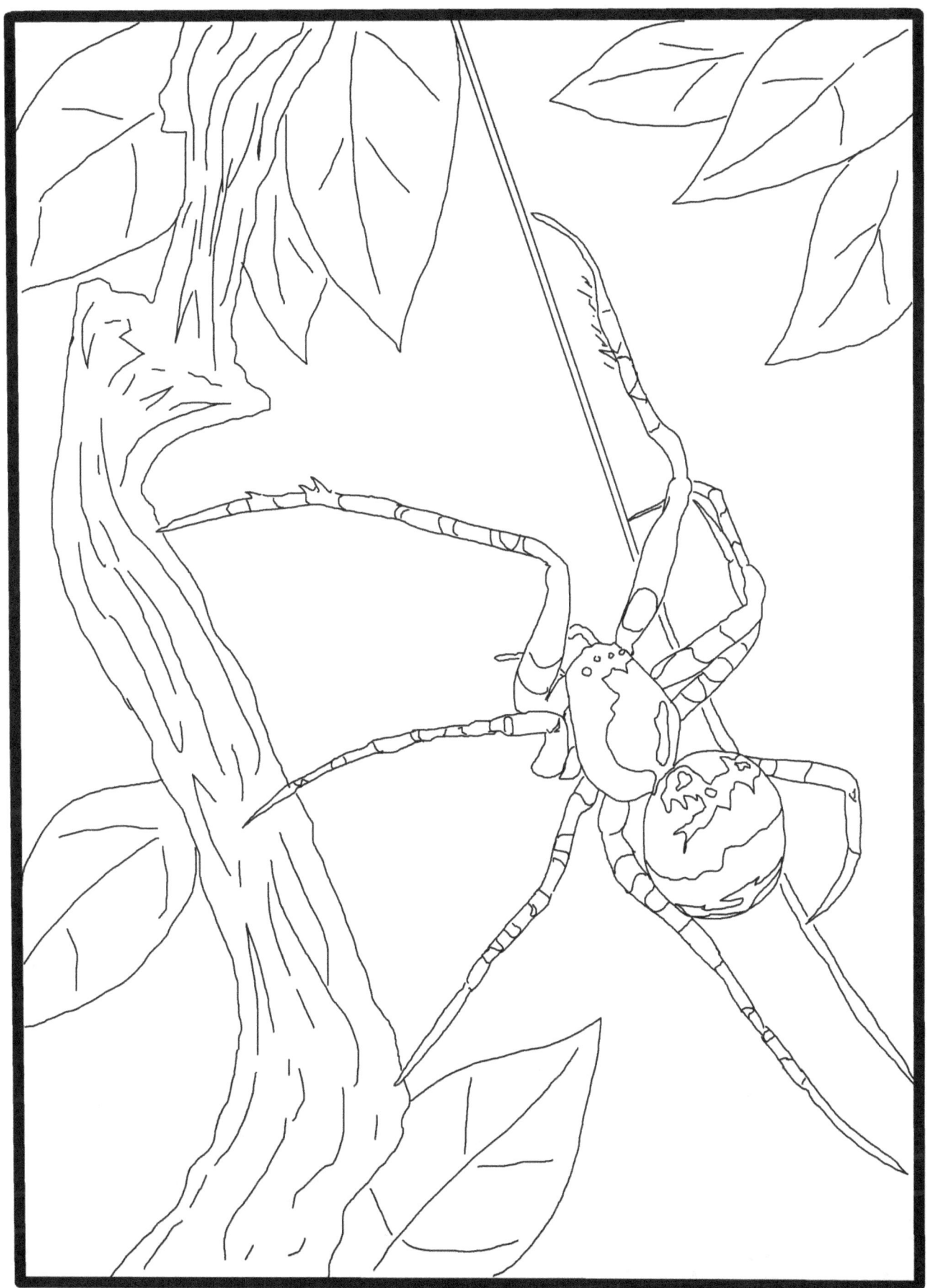

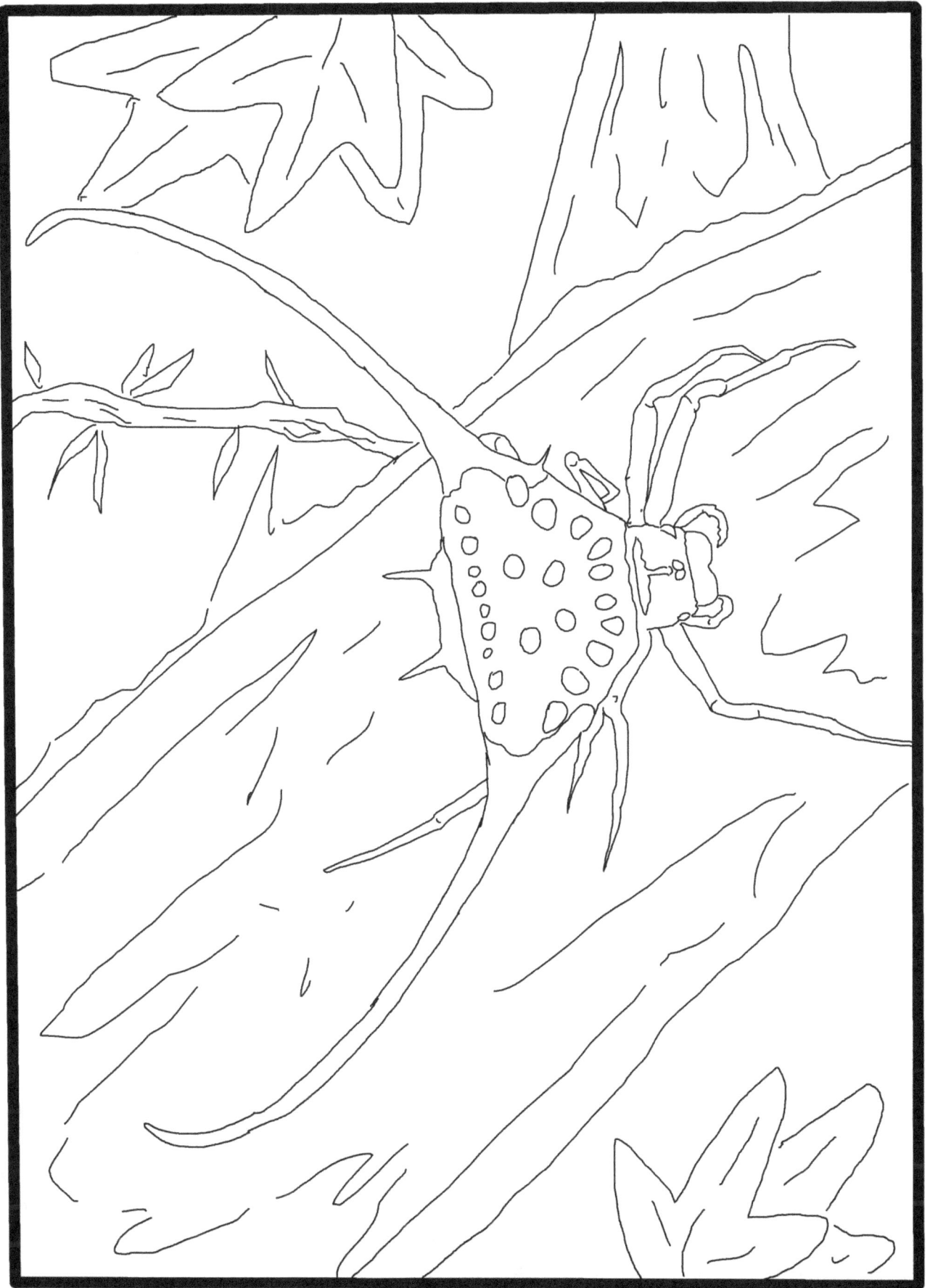

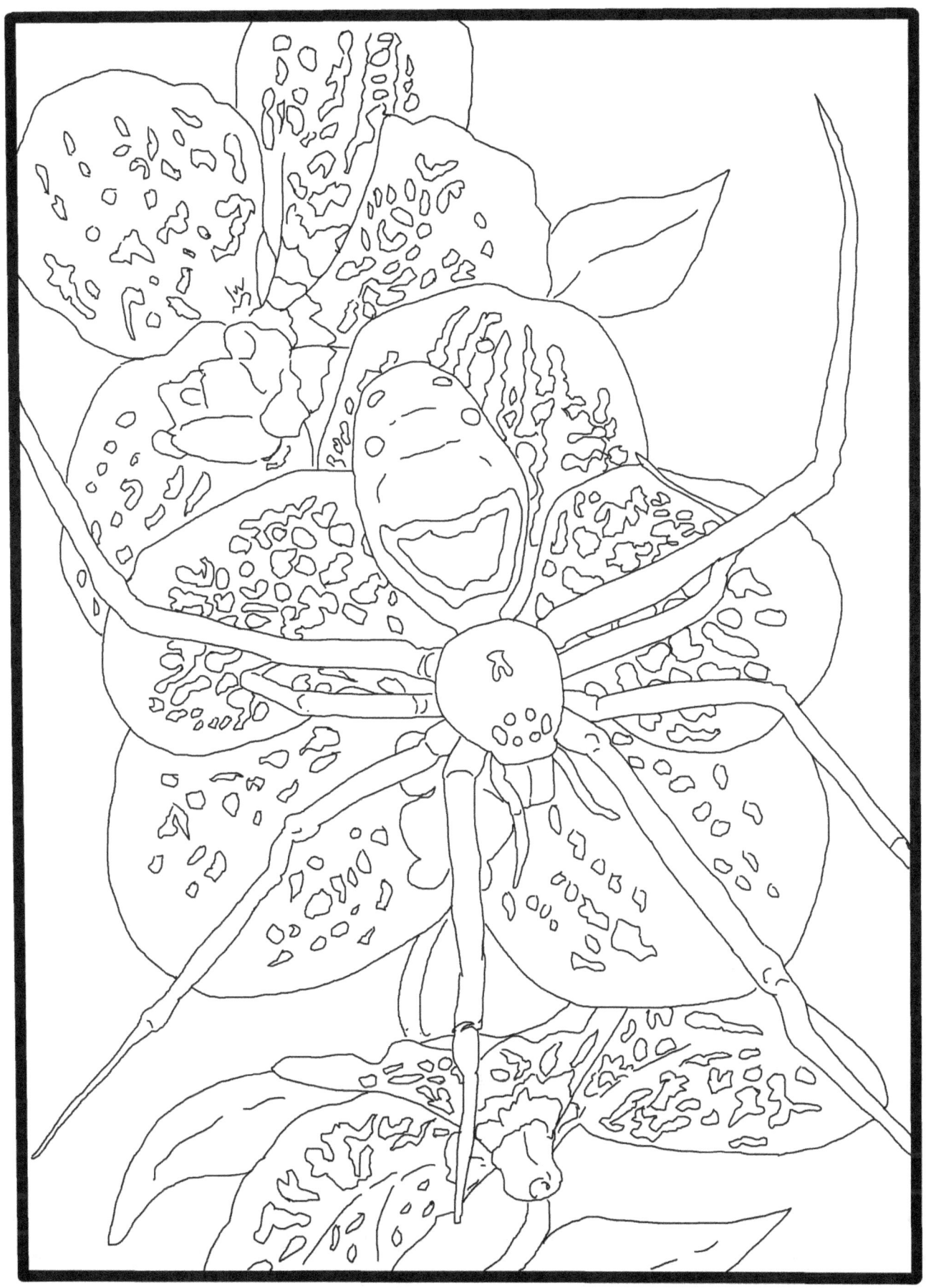

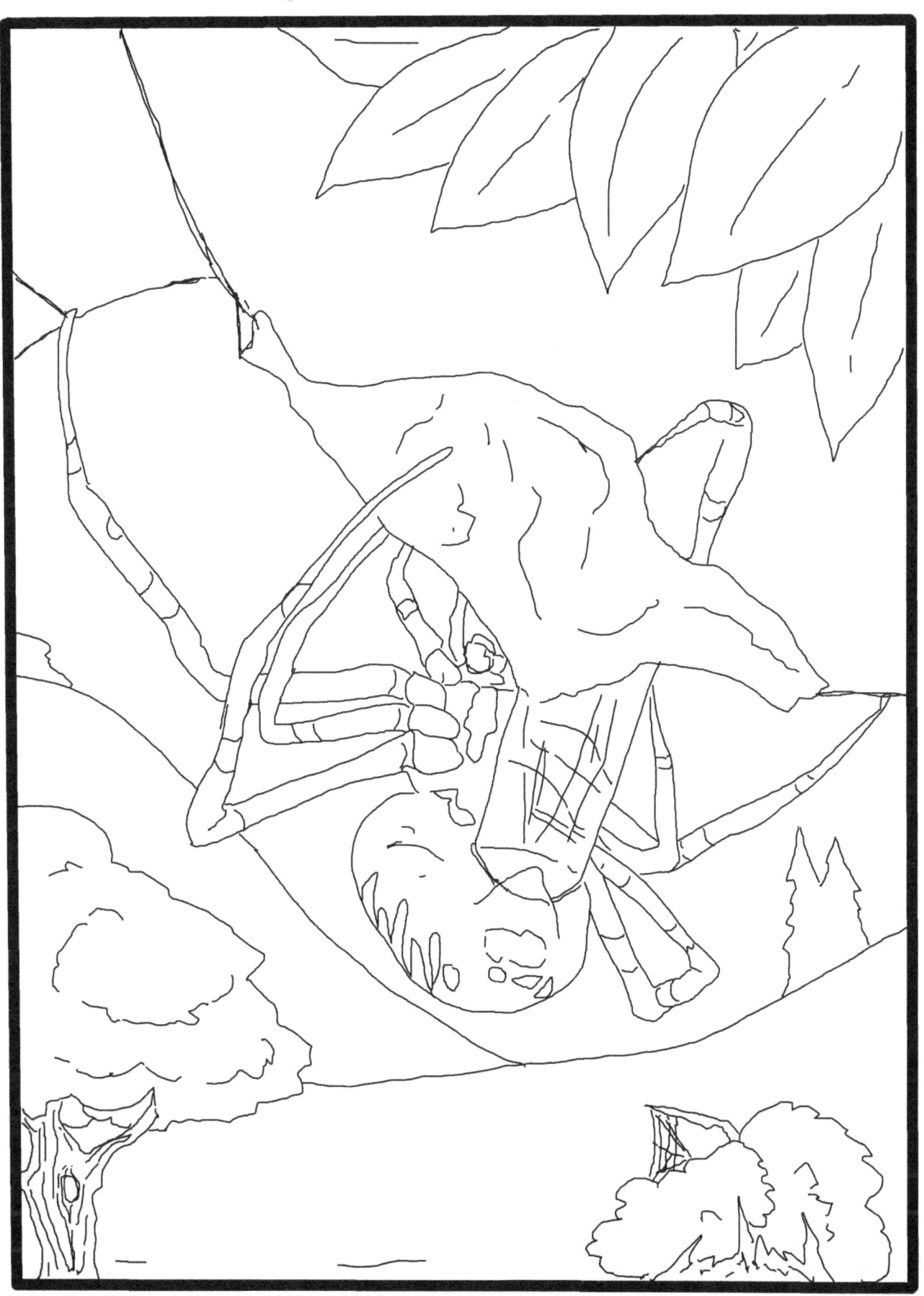

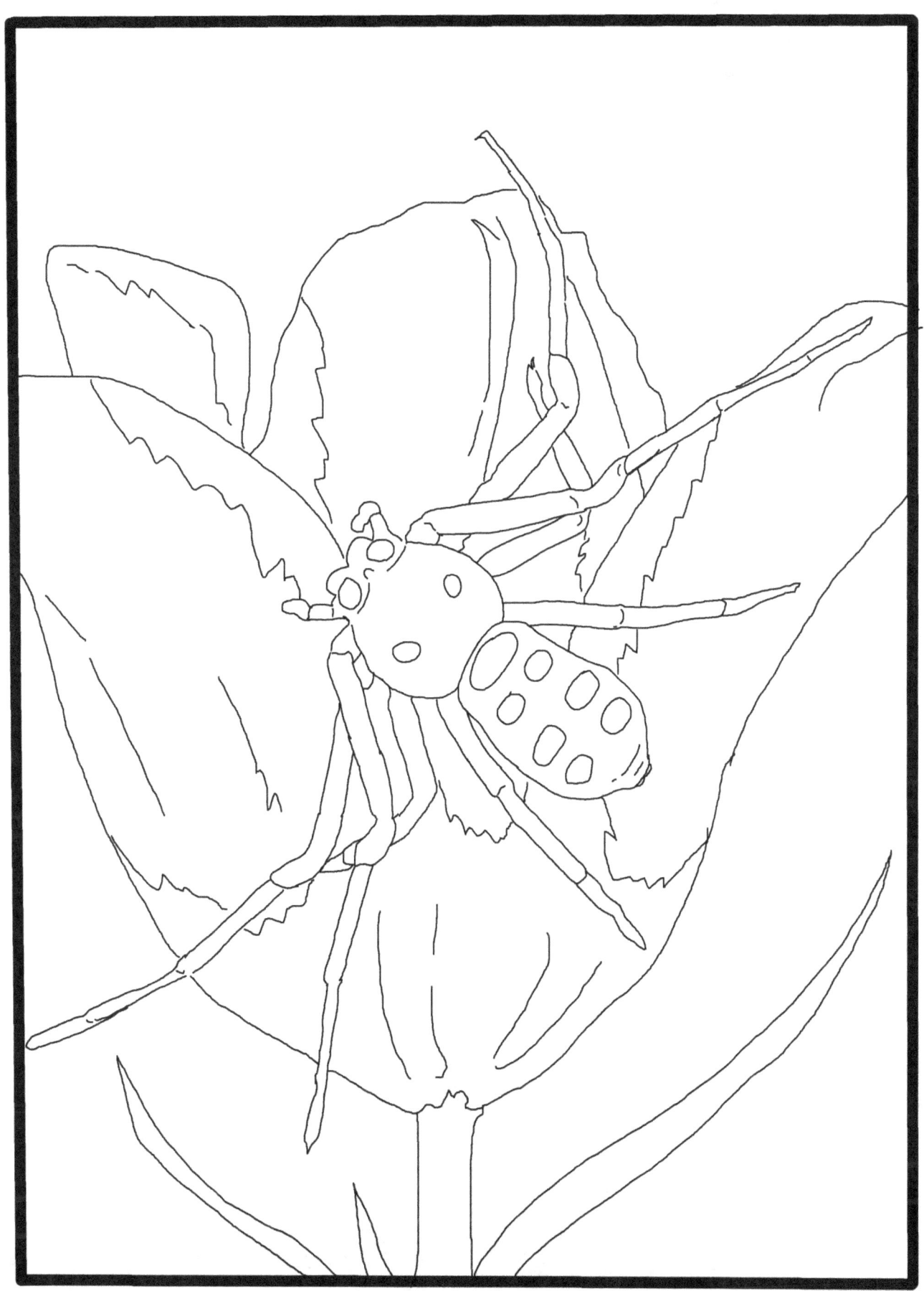

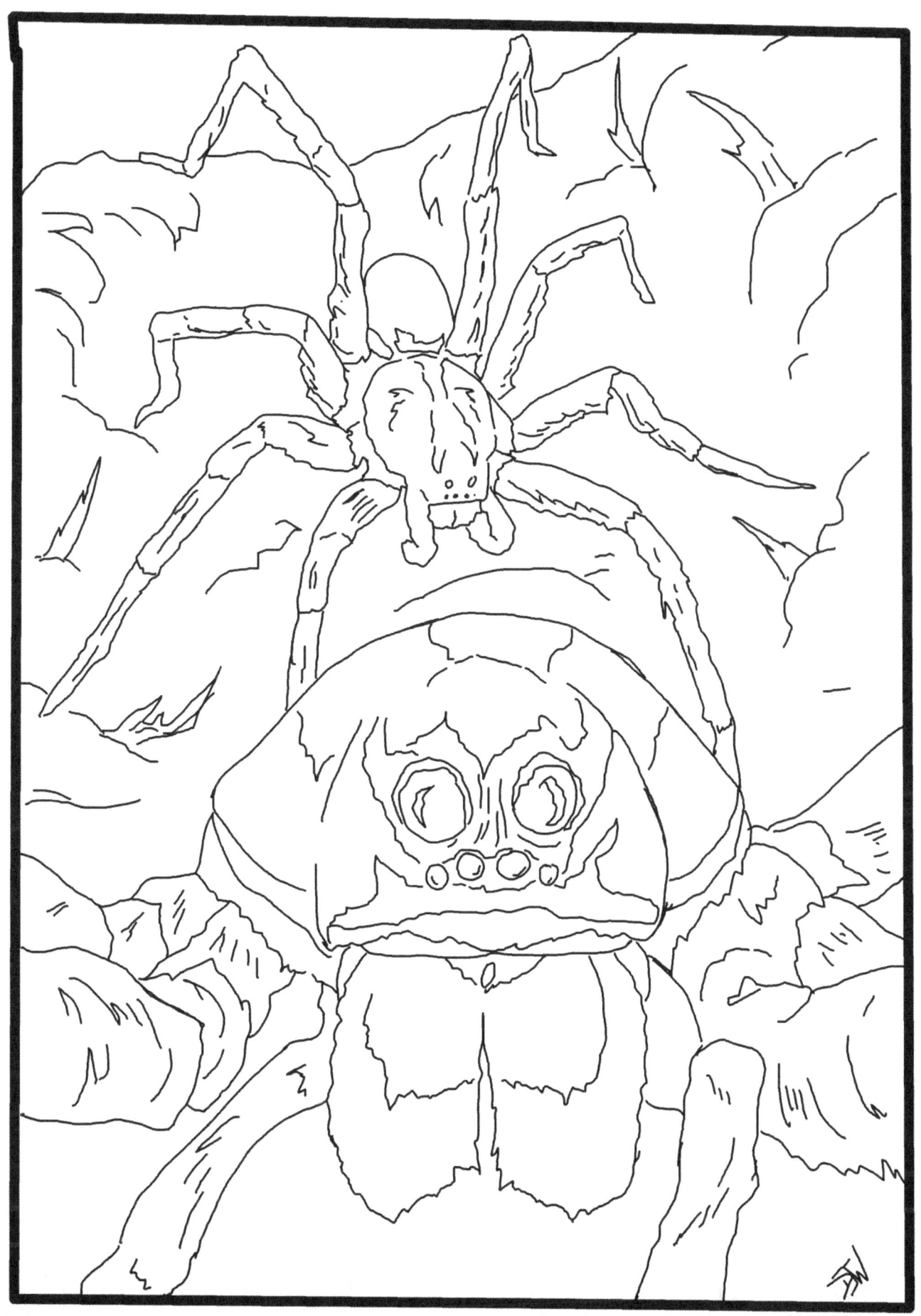